Stayin' Alive

Stayin'

Alive

the invention of safe sex
a personal history

Richard Berkowitz

Westview
PRESS

A Member of the Perseus Books Group

For the sake of privacy, names and identifying characteristics of some of those who appear in this book have been changed.

Westview Press books are available at special discounts for bulk purchases in the United States by corporations, institutions, and other organizations. For more information, please contact the Special Markets Department at the Perseus Books Group, 11 Cambridge Center, Cambridge MA 02142, or call (617) 252-5298 or (800) 255-1514 or email j.mccrary@perseusbooks.com.Published in the United States of America by Westview Press, 5500 Central Avenue, Boulder, Colorado 80301–2877 and in the United Kingdom by Westview Press, 12 Hid's Copse Road, Cumnor Hill,Oxford OX2 9JJ.

Find us on the World Wide Web at www.westviewpress.com

A Cataloging-in-Publication data record for this book is available from the Library of Congress.

ISBN 0-8133-4092-6

The paper used in this publication meets the requirements of the American National Standard for Permanence of Paper for Printed Library Materials Z39.48–1984.

10   9   8   7   6   5   4   3   2   1

To young gay men and women
struggling to keep sex safe.

Contents

Acknowledgments

I began writing this book in 1986, at the gnawing insistence of my dear, departed friend, Michael Callen. His death in 1993 catapulted me on a mission to get parts of this book published as articles in order to drum up interest in a publisher. After nine years, my only success came from a gay-run national magazine devoted exclusively to AIDS, which let me write five whole paragraphs about the history of safe sex. I knew something was wrong, but not what it was. Unable to comprehend the lack of interest, I searched myself for contributing factors. A form of survivor's guilt that began benignly—putting my needs aside to care for the sick and dying—had set in motion a process of self-obliteration that was being exploited by those around me, slowly reducing me to a buffoon, a doormat surrounded by eager, bitter feet. After a decade without interest in this history and nineteen years of condom diligence, I lost faith and gave up. The call to tell me I had a book contract came as I was walking into a hospital to be treated for my first-ever case of syphilis. A book meant to save others ended up saving me. Entering psychoanalysis, I realized at long last, it's enough.

Jill Rothenberg is the reason there is a first-hand account of how safe sex began. She believed in my voice when my ability had rusted, gently but persistently and always professionally prodding me along to catch up with her conviction. I'm grateful to her in a way that includes and exceeds writer to editor. I always will be.

The remaining acknowledgments fall into three main categories, the women, the deceased and miscellaneous.

Maria Scarfone leads the pack for sheer endurance, devotion and patience, endlessly reading and editing re-writes of these chapters since I began writing them. My sister and soul mate, this socialist "wench on wheels" and spiritual warrior has been ready to kick anyone's ass who got in my way since we were co-workers in 1978.

Barbara Serle-Rhodes has made me laugh more than anyone in the world, starting twenty-nine years ago when I needed it most. She still does. Her impact on my life is in everything I write.

Ardele Lister has been my sister and rabbi since I moved to Manhattan twenty-five years ago, helping me heal my wounded relationship to Judaism. To have a truly great artist in my personal life is a source of inspiration that's a precious gift. My insights about Judaism that appear in this book all come from her.

Celia Farber has made me realize what it means to be a journalist. No one I know understands the psychic scars from the battle for greater scrutiny of the truth better than she does. Grant applications and book proposals only ask for two samples of published work in a mainstream venue, but no one knew the only two I had were assignments she got for me in *SPIN*. When I'd reached the last lap of finishing this book and ran out of steam, Celia practically moved in with me until I got it back. She also tapped her friendship with a tenacious attorney to convince her to represent my interests in negotiating my book contract.

That most extraordinary attorney who fought for me and did so for a most-meager fee was Ruth Liebesman, Esq., to whom I'm truly indebted.

Norma Connolly, Esq. and Ronni Whitman have been unwavering in their belief in my writing and in me since our days together at Rutgers in the 1970s, rooting for me to keep reaching for a goal that after so many elusive years made others wince.

Michelle Cochrane, Ph.D., is one of the AIDS epidemic's best-kept secrets when it comes to jaw-dropping discoveries from her investigative journalism and revolutionary insights that inform her scholarly writing, which re-examines some of our most religiously held beliefs about AIDS. Her book, *Unraveling AIDS*, still pending publication, about the social construction of AIDS knowledge, will give the sun a case of illumination-envy when her work gets the exposure it deserves. Through the 1990s, her endurance in editing my articles that never got published enlightened a great deal of what is written about AIDS that appears here.

It was Ms. Cochrane who put me in touch with Ilene Kalish at Routledge, Inc., who read my book proposal and did what no one else did: generously offered me her wisdom about where to take it, leading me to Westview Press and peace at last. Thank you Ilene!

Who knew the best thing about being a gay man would be all the room that left in my life for a battalion of extraordinary women?

Writer Edmund White gave me invaluable advice when he referred me to the inimitable Patrick Merla, a generous, tireless advocate for struggling gay writers. His wise counsel in seeing me through the process of making a professional proposal was key in making this book happen.

Norman Macafee provided the most extraordinary copyediting of my manuscript that I'm deeply indebted to him for accomplishing.

Geoffrey F. Rose was my link to a new generation of young men and the ways that safe sex was failing them: "there's no rational middle ground between barebacking and wearing full latex sheets!" There's also nothing like the hope-filled eyes of a well-read, twenty-one-year-old brimming with self-esteem to energize a worn man like me. His bright, extensive editorial suggestions on every word of this book were invaluable.

During a difficult period, PEN American Center's Writers Fund Committee generously provided me with funds that matched the amount I requested. What a relief from the current American experience to have a place where a writer can get help, keep his dignity and not have to grovel or jump through endless hoops.

Various good friends have provided moral support, restaurant meals and some have helped me out in a financial pinch: Joe Guerro (for thirty years of free haircuts and happy beach memories), Joe Samler, Walter Newkirk, Louise Licata, Gloria G., Stephen Simon, Donald Adler, Sushuma, SALNYCTOP, Bill T., and most especially Paul H.

Richard Dworkin was Michael Callen's valiant lover and the unsung heroic editor of everything we wrote. I'm grateful to him for the years of advice and editing.

When the contract for this book finally came, I knew there was much to heal and I needed some serious psychiatric help; I got it from someone as brilliant as William Wedin, Ph.D., a clinical psychiatrist I once interviewed. After weeks of getting jerked around at hospitals, I called him. He had sufficient faith in me to believe this book would be a big enough success for me to be able to repay him one day and to have the integrity to do so.

At Westview Press I also want to thank Trish Goodrich and Greg Houle.

My greatest thanks goes to Dr. Joseph Sonnabend. Simply put, he is the reason I am alive and for that I am forever grateful.

Lastly, I wish to thank all my family for their love and support. Most of all, my Uncle Marvin who together with my late Aunt Stella, made me believe that money grows on trees. Without his endless support and unconditional love, I don't know how I would have made it through unendurable times.

It is in the memory of my beloved fallen friends that I dedicate this book: Rob. R, who taught me that I could love before I could fully appreciate its value; Richard E. Hendlowitch, the best friend I ever had and ever will; Michael Callen, my hero of heroes; Michael Lasarte; Dan Turner; Bobbi Campbell; Bobby Reynolds; Vito Russo; Tom Nasrallah; Artie F.; Mathew S.; Nicky; George H.; Lance Loud; Bobby Blume; Joe D. W.; Billie B.

And to one of my personal heroes, Robert Gould, M.D., in memory of all those who have suffered from our lack of civility in public discourse.

Introduction

last man standing

As I neared the completion of this book, a tragic realization struck me: I've lived in the fastest lane of sex in New York City since before AIDS began. Everyone I've known and loved and came out with in the 1970s is dead and gone. Everyone thinks they know what killed them.

With few exceptions, almost anything you will ever read about AIDS or about safe sex or about the gay community's response to this syndrome of diseases will be told with an immutable sense of victimhood, heroism, and pathos. The responses you are permitted to have will be predetermined: AIDS was nobody's fault. AIDS was a natural catastrophe that came from a clear blue sky and disproportionately struck gay men for no good or comprehensible reason. The gay community rallied and fought back in ways that render us virtually saintly. We got organized, we stood up, we chanted, we demanded answers, and we held the pharmaceutical industry, the Reagan administration, the media, and the world at large *accountable*. But for me, a crucial group was missed.

I am alive today because each step of the way, throughout the AIDS crisis, year after year, the advice I followed was different and often the opposite of what most gay men had been told to do. My life has never been so diminished by a single force as it has been by the catastrophe of AIDS. But none of my friends died from a disease or a syndrome of diseases. They didn't have the chance. They died from the other half of the catastrophe we've barely begun to wrap our minds around, the catastrophe of our human response to AIDS.

The almost unbearably tragic truth is that despite all the blaming and finger-pointing that we've done in all directions, we held the keys to survival the whole time. The answer wasn't complicated, fancy, high-tech, scientific, or costly. It was a set of commonsense rules that, if we had stuck to them from the start, would have saved countless lives and protected a new generation at risk. This is what I mean when I use the term "safe sex." Not the easy, MTV-friendly "safe sex" that you think of when you hear the term. This memoir is a history of not only the invention of safe sex, but a unique journey that escaped the systematic obliteration of it by a public relations–driven cadre of activists who distorted and co-opted the language, responses and the reality of AIDS from the beginning.

On the 20th anniversary of the invention of safe sex, *Stayin' Alive* recounts the journey that led me to become a driving force behind the invention of safe sex. Not as I wish it had been, not how it should have been, but how it was. This is not the whole history of safe sex, it's just mine.

Much has been written about AIDS, but little about its crucial prehistory. Many people think AIDS began in May 1983, when America awoke, rolled up its sleeves, and immediately wanted to know who was to blame but not who needed care. Nearly two years, however, had already gone by in which people were dying, activists were pleading for help, and hardly anyone cared. Having witnessed that period, I realized while watching America waking up to AIDS that my country's reaction was exactly what activists had predicted and prepared for. With their world collapsing all around them and their lives in peril, why not lie to those who didn't care if you lived? Truth became a thing to manage; it needed a makeover. Sometimes the truth we get is the truth we ask for, but the problem is, we never know who might later suffer from such compromises to the truth. I see a new generation paying the price of equivocations and distortions.

In August 1982, I arrived on the frontlines in the war against AIDS, having just ended a lucrative career as an S&M hustler. Following the sensible ideas of my physician, Dr. Joseph Sonnabend, prevented me from joining the predominantly gay AIDS establishment of that time. As a result, I discovered a sea of hope that few others saw, which made me feel I could save my own life, which in turn made adapting to safe sex a breeze. The AIDS establishment hinged their every utterance on the core idea that AIDS was something you either caught or didn't. Russian roulette. A worldwide case of the cooties. My perspective, handed to me from the start by Dr. Joseph Sonnabend, is that AIDS is often something that you develop over time or from more than a single causative factor. This idea was intolerable to the Gatekeepers of AIDS Information. It implied there was another group that had to be held accountable: ourselves. That would have demanded a more truthful and unsentimental look at post–gay liberation sexuality and its biological realities. I understood how dangerous and difficult that would have been, which is why to an extent I forgive those tactics. At the time, the media and general public were a virtual lynch mob of anti-gay contempt, screaming that we deserved to die of AIDS. In this bloodthirsty climate, how could gay people be expected to be candid? I understand, but my forgiveness ends with a new generation's increasingly ominous infection rates.

I'm not interested in assigning blame or naming names. I don't know of anyone, including me, who has worked on AIDS issues who hasn't made mistakes. But I did something right to still be here. Never being confused about the relevance, importance, and definition of safe sex is a large part of that. However, little else in my life has left me feeling so alone. The only way I could cope was to stop talking about it, not with people in general, but always with gay men. Nothing I could say would clear up the confusion over the ever-changing definitions of safe sex that demoralized many gay men who genuinely believed uncertainty was unavoidable. I didn't; I believed that to some degree, we had been betrayed by some of those in whom we had placed our trust.

Knowing what safe sex is and what safe sex isn't is a matter of life and death for those at risk, but guidelines have been dizzying. Determining which particular sex acts belonged in high risk columns and low risk columns changed from brochure to brochure, organization to organization, year to year. Throughout the 1980s, Gay Men's Health Crisis re-defined safe sex almost every time they redesigned their brochures. Then came the creation of more categories. Added to high risk and low risk, came "medium risk," "unknown risk" and the ever-popular "risk not yet determined." More categories led to even more bouncing around from one column of risk to another. Anal sex with a condom became an endless back and forth dance, from high risk to medium risk to low risk to possibly safe. What were sexually active gay men supposed to do? Oral sex did the same dance soon after. What faith could gay men have in safe sex when so few agreed on what it was for long? It is my belief that some confusion was intentionally generated for the purpose of undermining confidence in safe sex. There were those among us who were infuriated that AIDS didn't lead gay men to embrace monogamy. Some accused Dr. Sonnabend, late activist Michael Callen and me of "promoting promiscuity" when we published our safe sex manifesto, which was produced, in part, because we recognized that there were those who were continuing to engage in unprotected sex with multiple partners despite AIDS. Like the abortion debate, safe sex was a choice that some didn't want gay men to have. But instead of choosing monogamy when safe sex began to be undermined by dueling studies that reached different conclusions, justifications to abandon safe sex were found. For example, once you're HIV positive, why does safe sex matter? Isn't it too late? Lost in a blizzard of confusion, contradictory study findings and uncertainty, it was just a matter of time until unsafe sex came out of the shadows with a pent-up rage.

Having been involved in the invention of safe sex, I was fortunate not to be distracted by confusion. I knew what it was: don't get sperm inside your rectum.

I was a product of the sexual exuberance of the 1970s, but I never knew the meaning of sexual freedom until I adopted safe sex practices to adapt to the age of AIDS and discovered a decade later that I had largely escaped many other sexually transmitted infections that are their own tyranny. Being surrounded by years of unspeakable suffering and death fortified my determination to keep sex safe. A new generation can't imagine what that was like. They hear that AIDS is a manageable disease without understanding that what is being managed is death.

This book fulfills promises I made to friends as they lay dying, to never give up until the story of how and why safe sex was invented and how it went awry was recorded for the new and for future generations.

Several times in the early 1990s, when death drew near for one of my longtime friends with AIDS, signaling the time to tell me good-bye, there was a moment of disbelief when they'd look at me and say, "I can't believe I'm dying and *you're* still here!" They'd shake their head in disbelief or muster a faint laugh through a morphine haze and proceed to make sure one last time that I understood my sentencing. "It's not just your story, it's my story, too, to tell the next generation. If they don't like the truth . . . fuck 'em. Tell them we didn't like it, either. Tell them how much more they won't like it ending up like this. Tell them we promised to come back and haunt you if you didn't tell this story."

I can smile about it now; I couldn't then. I stood there, not saying a word about why I was still there: two little words (safe sex) and three lethal letters (AZT). Today, doses of AZT are a fraction of what was prescribed in the early '90s, but what hasn't changed is how easily HIV infection can enslave an unfettered life and turn it into a lifelong science project. The list of serious side effects of drugs used today in combination *therapy is still growing*. That's no cure.

To honor a vow I made to Michael Callen, with whom I wrote the first safe sex manifesto, *How to Have Sex in an Epidemic: One Approach,* I have crammed as much graphic and salacious sexual detail as I reasonably could into this story about safe sex. Unfortunately for my family, most of it is mine; Michael gave the remainder to me with the words "Use any and all of it as you wish."

This book began as Michael's idea, which he instilled in me as a duty. The day after he died, his lawyer called me to read a section of Michael's will. I was so moved as I waited to hear what it was that Callen wanted me to have:

"To Richard Berkowitz, I leave a swift kick in the butt every time he gets writer's block. The history of safe sex is important for the next generation. It's up to him now to see it done."

Dialogue sections that appear are based on conversations I recorded, which were often beset by interruptions, meandering digressions, inaudible gaps, etc. What appears is edited, condensed for clarity, pieced together from multiple conversations as well as reconstructed ones from notes, personal diaries and my best recollection. Callen reviewed most of his text before he died in December 1993. *Stayin' Alive* is a New York–based story; it does not reflect what was happening elsewhere.

1

Coming Out in the '70s

a journey from
childhood to promiscuity

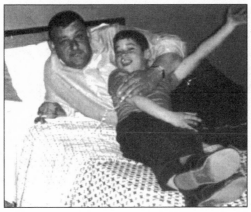

Richard, age 7, with Dad

I was born October 6, 1955, in Newark, New Jersey, and raised in a working-class apartment complex in the nearby suburb of Union. Our town had a slogan proclaiming on signs at intersections: "What helps youth, helps Union." But no one knew how to help a boy who loved singing, dancing, and shopping but couldn't care less about the obsession with sports that defined boyhood, especially in the late 1950s and early 1960s. It's hard to believe that a carefree, seven-year-old could pose a threat to the social order, but when a boy is perceived as a "sissy," he does. To save me from a boy's worst fate, adults stepped in to tone me down and butch me up.

But before the gender police intervened, I was a happy, oblivious kid. I grew up with two older brothers who loved and protected me. As one of my earliest childhood memories attests, they
also understood me. One night in a fancy restaurant a hostess
greeted my family's table by asking, "Three boys but no girls?"

"We came close with Richie," my mischievous brother Bruce
explained. We cracked up laughing at the look on that lady's face as
soon as she scurried away.

I never learned how to play sports or how to fight. I didn't
want to or have to; I had two big brothers who defended me
against bullies. They told me that I was the lucky son: By the time I
came along, my parents were too old and tired to enforce all the
rules my brothers had lived by. Boys were strong, not weak, tough
not emotional, and in the arena of life they strove to be the winner.
I couldn't find my happiness in that.

I had two aunts and an uncle, none of whom married. Each
treated me like the child they might have had. Aunt Sylvia graduated law school in the 1930s. Aunt Stella and Uncle Marvin had
master's degrees. They taught me about Jewish customs and history, about my family's roots in Russia and Austria, about
pogroms and the Holocaust. I loved listening to stories of how
my grandparents immigrated to America and about all my ances-
tors they left behind. Since most of them were dead, stories were
all we had.

My parents were always very affectionate with each other;
Aunt Stella called them "two contented cows in love." Their mutual devotion gave me a feeling of security as the 1960s wore on
and many of my friends' parents were divorcing. Whether we were
in the station wagon going on car trips or plopped down in front of
the TV, my father was constantly caressing my mother's arms,
making me feel safe from change.

In the fall of 1963, though, life suddenly turned serious and
my idyllic childhood came to an end. My grandmother's death left

my mother's family in such a deep state of mourning, I thought their grief would never go away. Two months later, President Kennedy was assassinated and suddenly it seemed that the whole world was mourning. In the midst of all that sadness, I caused a third-grade scandal that I couldn't understand, but nothing after that would ever be the same. My mother had told me to invite my friends to my eighth birthday party, and over twenty-five kids showed up. But when my teacher got wind of the mixed-gender guest list, my mother was summoned to the principal's office. At my school boy/girl parties were not supposed to happen until sixth grade, but at my party girls outnumbered boys because most of my friends were girls. After her meeting, my mother began scolding me for things I always did, but now all of a sudden they were wrong, like talking with my hands on my hips, or stinking up the apartment because I kept spraying too much Pledge, and if Mike is playing Roy Rogers who else is left but Dale Evans and it wasn't a dress it was a dish towel.

I learned about the gender line that separated boys and girls from the consequences of having crossed it, but altering my behavior was like rewrapping a package; it didn't change what was inside it just taught me that I had to hide it. But as the saying goes, some things are easier said than done.

One Sunday night my family and I were watching *The Ed Sullivan Show* when the Beatles performed. I became so excited by all the screaming girls in the audience; they expressed exactly what I was feeling—a wild love for the Beatles. During their performance, there was a close-up of John Lennon and a subtitle appeared saying, "Sorry girls, John is married." I screamed in disappointment: John was taken. My parents were surprised by my reaction, but it probably prepared them for what came next.

There were photos of the Fab Four on all their record jackets and I'd always take a pencil, circle their faces and, like a beauty pageant judge, number them in order of how cute I thought they looked. I became the first Beatle-banged obsessed boy in Franklin Grammar School. I loved being a trendsetter.

One Friday morning I couldn't get my hair combed right. Suddenly, the bathroom door flew open. My mother was standing there fuming, but I was too engrossed to care.

"I thought you left. What the hell are you doing? You're already late!"

As I bent over the sink for one more stab at getting my bangs to lay straight, my mother grabbed me in a rage that I'd never seen before.

"You're *a boy,* damn it! You're not supposed to care how your hair looks!" She snatched my arm and marched me out the front door. "I don't know what I'm gonna do with you! You're not *normal!*" In tears, she slammed the door shut behind me.

I felt so humiliated I couldn't stop crying as I walked to school. Wasn't I a good kid? I never got into trouble, I got good grades, and I helped out with chores at home a lot more than most kids. Uncle Marvin even taught me how to sew and iron my shirts to perfection. What was I doing that was so awful, that sparked such a fury in my mom? I worried that something about me was evil, but I couldn't figure out what it was.

After school, I wanted to run away. Instead, I called my Aunt Stella and Uncle Marvin, my mother's unmarried brother and sister who lived together in Newark, and I invited myself over.

They became my refuge that weekend and almost every weekend and holiday thereafter until I went away to college. In their house I was free to be myself again. I could stand in front of the mirror and play with my hair, sing and dance to my Beatles records or do whatever I wished. Pizza at 1 A.M.? "Sure." Cookies for breakfast? "Why not?" Can I try on Aunt Stella's wigs and jewelry? "Have fun."

When I was eleven, my family moved from our overcrowded apartment into a three-bedroom, split-level house. Since my father was a bricklayer and mason, he laid a huge patio in the backyard.

After all the cement was poured and meticulously smoothed over, my father got down on his knees and scratched deep into the corner of the patio, "MILT LOVES DOTTY."

When my mother came to the window and saw what he'd done, her face lit up with such joy that mine did too. As I stood there watching the eye contact exchanged between my parents, I tried to imagine doing something like that for my wife someday, but I drew a blank. I couldn't see myself as a husband with a wife. Maybe like my aunts and uncle, I was going to be one of those people who never married. In spite of three such wonderful role models, I felt so sad. I couldn't stand the thought of being alone.

My brothers told me that on the days of their bar mitzvahs, the Jewish ceremony marking a boy's transition to manhood, my father took them into the master bedroom and told them the facts of life. Bruce had already told me everything I wanted to know about sex and I felt uncomfortable anticipating "the talk." I wanted my dad to know he could skip it, but to my surprise, I was even more uncomfortable when he did. Instead of talking about birds and bees, we ended up discussing fish.

"You know, Richie, it seems like we don't have enough things we do in common because you're not interested in sports—and that's okay. People aren't all the same and that's what makes the world go around. But we should find something we could do to spend more time together, just you and me, like a hobby or—"

"I would love an aquarium with all different kinds of tropical fish."

That afternoon my dad took me to a discount store and bought me a ten-gallon tank, the prettiest fish in the store and books about how to care for them. My dad and I had found a hobby that brought us closer together. But I wondered why I was the only son he never told the facts of life to. My dad knew something was different about me, but he navigated his love for me around it and left the messy work of dealing with it to Mom.

Sex popped up all around me that year I turned thirteen, and it wasn't like I went looking for it—it kept coming after me. On the first day of eighth grade, two handsome hooligans, who looked destined for a life dealing in contraband, took me aside in gym class. "We can get sperm. Come over after school and we'll show you." I was aroused but horrified. They were so tough, they bullied the boys who bullied me.

I was afraid to meet them but nothing could stop me. I sat on the floor of one of their bedrooms with my pulse racing, cotton-mouthed and paralyzed by a level of desire I'd never known before. I knew they wanted me to "play the girl" but I was too terrified. The next day I was so touched when they showed up at my back-yard with plants for my garden. For bad boys, they were being so sweet. Then they mentioned that they'd stolen all the plants from neighbors' backyards. I felt guilty planting them in our garden but relieved by their gifts for sexual favors not rendered.

My friend Eric was a different story. We'd known each other since third grade. Years later when I told him that one of my broth-ers was accumulating stacks of *Playboy* and *Penthouse* magazines in our bedroom closet, Eric came running over to see them. After checking out the latest acquisitions, Eric said he wanted to "fool around." Mutual masturbation eventually led to awkward oral sex, which continued for five years, until we went away to college.

"This doesn't mean we're homosexuals," Eric was careful to explain, since it was his idea. "It's just a substitute because we're too young to mess with girls." That sounded fine to me, but I could no longer ignore my blossoming attraction to boys.

Bruce's magazines mainly frustrated me. After school, I'd lock myself in the bathroom with a stack of copies. There were thou-sands of pictures of naked people but none of them were men! The erotic power of what little I did find, like *Playboy's* men's fash-ion layouts, was hypnotic, but as soon as I climaxed I was overcome with guilt and shame. One moment writhing in ecstasy, the next moment cringing in disgrace, all that pleasure instantly drowned by feeling sick and dirty. I vowed to masturbate while looking at pictures of naked women, but never got around to it. While scanning past hundreds of pictures of beautiful females, my dick was dead until I came across a handsome man.

My parents openly declared my brother's interest in pictures of naked women, and by implication, masturbation, to be "healthy and normal, nothing shameful or to hide." But I knew that if they discovered what was fueling my fantasies they'd be so ashamed *they'd* run and hide. I was sure of that from a story my mother told us one night at dinner about a homosexual hangout in town at a rest area on the Garden State Parkway.

"Your father took me out for coffee last night to Howard Johnson's and the place was infested with 'faygalas.' It's so sad, men trying to be women without the proper plumbing."

"Stop! We're trying to eat," my brothers pleaded as their visible visceral disgust shook me to my bones.

"One of them kept trying to braid his ponytail so I went over and taught him how to do it. You have to feel sorry for men like that, they're just sick. Do you know what your father said? 'It's a tragedy, because men like that will never know the love of a good woman.' And I couldn't help but think, for each one of them there's a mother somewhere with a broken heart wondering what she did wrong. Thank you God for blessing me with three boys who will never put me through that. It would just kill me."

I excused myself abruptly from the table and hurried upstairs to the bathroom. I threw up what I'd eaten and broke down crying as I sank to the bathroom floor, the site of my unrelenting shame. I begged God with all my might to help me change, but the next day I was back on the same spot, panting over a shirtless hockey player pictured in *Life* magazine. I quivered. I climaxed. I felt doomed.

In 1969, *Everything You Always Wanted to Know About Sex but Were Afraid to Ask,* by David Reuben, M.D., became a number-one best-seller and a media sensation. Dr. Reuben became a celebrity, appearing on TV shows. My parents left a copy in the night table next to their bed. Finally, I had access to a book explaining what I was going through written in an easy-to-read, question-and-answer format.

"Couldn't homosexuals just be born that way?"

"A lot of homosexuals would like to think so. They prefer to consider their problem the equivalent of a club-foot or birthmark, just something to struggle through life with. This explanation is a little tragic. It implies that all homosexuals are condemned without appeal to a life some of them they say they enjoy so much. Actually for those who want to change there is a chance."

"How?"

"If a homosexual who wants to renounce his homo-sexuality finds a psychiatrist who knows how to cure homosexuality, he has every chance of becoming a happy, well-adjusted, heterosexual."

Thank God, I thought, there's hope. There *is* a cure. Dr. Reuben continued.

"Homosexuals are trying the impossible: solving the problem with only half the pieces. They say they want sexual gratification and love but they eliminate . . . the most obvious source of love and gratification—woman. Tragically, there is no possibility of satisfaction because the formula is wrong. One penis plus one penis equals nothing."

"What about all the homosexuals who live together happily for years?"

"What about them? They are mighty rare birds among the homosexual flock. Moreover, the 'happy' part remains to be seen . . . Live together? Yes. Happily? Hardly."[1]

Now I knew this sickness inside me could end. All I had to do was keep it hidden until I could afford a doctor who could teach me how to make it go away.

Ninth grade brought torture into my life in the form of Algebra 1 class. To make matters worse, I broke my arm playing football in gym class and missed so much school my mother had to arrange for an algebra tutor to help me catch up.

Near the end of our first session, I noticed my tutor staring between my legs. I peeked over and realized his palm kept pressing down on his crotch. I clamped my legs together and rested my hands over my zipper, but the warmth and weight of my hands conspired to make me hard. Clashing waves of repulsion and desire washed over me. I wanted to run. I wanted him to touch me. I felt nauseous. I felt aroused. The back-and-forth conflict between desire and disgrace settled onto a yearning for him to just hold me and tell me that somehow my life would turn out okay.

He took my hand and slowly placed it on his crotch, then reached over and began rubbing mine. As I stared at my textbook, I could feel my cheeks flushing red. Suddenly the doorbell rang. It was my mother returning early to take me home. As he jumped up to let her in, my face felt like it was on fire. I got up and ran outside.

"What's wrong with you?" my mother asked as she got into the car.

I couldn't look her in the eye. I was worried that she'd seen us through the window. I couldn't hesitate or she'd think I was trying to hide it. "He's homosexual."

"That *bastard!* He molested you? Tell me exactly what happened."

My fear was paranoia; she had no idea what had transpired. I had to carefully pick every word because only he and I knew I had become aroused. Who would people believe—the innocent 13-year-old or the middle-aged pervert? I erased my erection from my memory. It had never happened.

When we got home, my mother ran to the phone and called her girlfriends. I wanted to tell her to shut up about it, but I was afraid it would look like I had something to hide. And then I overheard her tell someone that the tutor had been previously fired from a school for molesting a boy. She had known that when she took me to his house.

I called my friend Eric to sort out what had happened.

"Rich, calm down, it's not like you got raped. What's the big deal? I bet he would have given you a great blow job."

For one brief crazy moment, what happened didn't seem so terrible. But Eric knew he liked girls. He had no idea how tormented I was about my homosexual desires.

"But if your mom knew he molested a boy, maybe she was testing you, so it's better you told her what happened or she might think you were a gay."

Think? Here was a lifelong friend I was having sex with maybe once a month and I couldn't even talk to him about my true feelings.

Over the next few weeks, my mother launched a campaign to destroy that tutor, telling her tale of woe to anyone who'd listen. I began to feel sorry for him. Although it was, ironically, the year that gay liberation was born, being a homosexual in 1969 in our town was the worst thing a man could be. As one of our neighbors said,

"They're not people—they're a disease." By "they" did he mean molesters or homosexuals? I knew not to ask. Being gay was so disgusting one didn't need to bother distinguishing between adult consensual gay sex and the molestation of a minor.

In 1970, when I turned fifteen, Aunt Stella started taking me to Puerto Rico and Miami during school vacations. At night I loved going out walking. What's the point of having a gorgeous suntan but to go out and show it off. Whether it was the Condado section of San Juan or the quiet streets between Collins Avenue and the ocean in Miami Beach, it was mind-boggling how I always found the places where men were looking for sex with other men. Thousands of miles from home where nobody knew me, I could sample my forbidden desires. I got blown but I never reciprocated. Fags were the cocksuckers; real men got their dicks sucked.

October of my senior year in high school brought good tidings. I turned seventeen, got my driver's license, and best of all, was notified of my early acceptance by Rutgers University. That was a dream come true. My dad was drowning in bills and the state university fees were half of my brothers' tuitions at out-of-state colleges. I was as good as done with high school, with eight months left to coast. My parents agreed I had earned the ride without realizing it was going to be a roller coaster.

The day my license arrived in the mail was my emancipation from the tedious boredom of being a teenager trapped at home. I paced our driveway waiting for my dad to return from work so I could take his car. There was only one place I wanted to go—Howard Johnson's on the Parkway. Not the one in Union, that was too close to home, but the one in Bloomfield wasn't and I'd heard it was just as "infested." I pulled into the Bloomfield rest area parking lot and saw a lot of cars at the far end with men sitting alone in them and the motors running. I picked a spot and pulled in. I fiddled with the radio, kept adjusting the rearview mirror, rummaged

through papers on the dashboard, organized the glove compart-
ment and pretended I was reading. Finally, I mustered the courage
to turn my head and gaze around as if looking was a felony.

Minutes turned to hours, and nothing was happening. Occa-
sionally I saw men get out of their cars and talk to each other; some
left, one car following the other out. Under the tall, bent streetlights
that shed a dim orange glow over the lot I noticed a young guy pull
in. I lowered my window and turned my head, hoping he'd see me.

As his car approached, three teenagers stuck their heads out
the windows. "Fucking queers! Get out of here, you sick faggots!"

Queers? Faggots? What was I doing here? I turned the key to
start the engine, but an awful grating noise reminded me it was already running. I put the car in reverse and almost hit a man walking by. As he yelled furiously at me, I tore out of the lot and back
onto the Parkway. I felt like people in the passing cars knew where
I'd just come from and why I was there. I pulled off at the first exit
and into the parking lot of a 7-Eleven. I went inside and bought my
first pack of cigarettes. I was a nervous wreck.

The following night, as soon as I pulled in, I got out of the car
and went into the Howard Johnson's to buy a coffee so that the
other men could see me. In no time at all, two cars had pulled up
next to mine and both men kept trying to get my attention. I felt
soaked in sexual desire but too paranoid to speak.

On the third night, as I started to relax, a cop car pulled into
the lot. Against my whispered prayers, he drove right to me, shin-
ing a blinding light through my dad's car.

"Driver's license and registration," the state trooper said in a you-
eat-shit tone. I pulled out my wallet and accidentally spilled most of
its contents all over my lap. As I picked up the papers and pictures, an
unexpected feeling of anger came over me. I wasn't doing anything
wrong that anyone could prove and so I resented the intimidation.

"What're you doing here?"

"I stopped in for a drink."

"Your cup's empty, so move on. There's no loitering in the parking lot."

As I drove away, I felt a smirk cross my face. Being bad felt good. I turned up the radio, lit a cigarette and thought, "I've worked hard to be what everyone expected of me. In ten months I'm going away to Rutgers to buckle down with my studies, find a girl to marry and have kids. Maybe I can't picture it but what's the alternative—being a middle-aged man cruising seedy parking lots all night long? This is my time to sow my wild oats and get this gay stuff out of my system once and for all."

September and the beginning of college would be my deadline to stop this and move on. I didn't need a doctor to cure me, all I had to do was think about how being a fag would devastate my family. But for colorful adventure and endless opportunities for blow jobs, the gay netherworld was a fascinating place to visit for a while. With that in perspective and a deadline to stop, I was able to let go of my post-orgasmic self-loathing.

By spring I was a regular at HoJo's. Now when I drove in, there were so many guys I'd gotten to know from chatting, sex was secondary. Being seventeen made me a novelty and the other regulars—most of whom were ten to thirty years older—were nice to me. Life at home, however, was becoming untenable. It was the same screaming routine with my mother seven nights a week.

"Where the hell were you till four o'clock in the morning?"

"Out."

"Out with *who*? What bums do you know who stay out this late?"

"Eric?"

"Liar! Eric called here looking for you. What are you hiding? Why are you lying to me all the time? If you're doing drugs I swear you'll never leave this house again."

"Check my pupils. Smell my clothes. Do I look like I'm on drugs?"

"I can smell you're smoking cigarettes. What's gotten into you, it's scaring me."

"I'm celebrating that I worked my ass off to get into Rutgers, tuition at half price."

"You're killing me away with worry and you don't even care."

But of course I cared. I also knew a liar was better than a faggot.

After a shower to get ready for another night out, my pubic hair was itching so badly I dug my hairbrush into it until I began to bleed. I felt an itch on my wrist and as I inspected it, I saw a tiny black thing twitch. It was alive! I screamed.

My parents came running. Hysterical, I tried to explain but my father interrupted.

"Crabs. I had them once in the army. We'll call the pharmacy and find out what you need to get rid of them."

As I carried all my clothes and bedding to the washing machine in the basement, my mother asked, "Where were you laying that you picked up crabs?"

I wasn't in the mood for verbal warfare. Live bugs had been growing on my body. I felt itchy and diseased down to my soul. Crabs ended sowing my oats.

The first cool evenings of late August always make me melancholy. Growing up, I'd spent every August at the Jersey shore. These were the happiest times of my youth, and I always felt sad when that first fall chill signaled the time to go home. But this year, for the first time, I was leaving home and the sadness cut deeper. I was terrified of leaving Aunt Stella, Uncle Marvin, and my parents and living in a dormitory with a secret to hide. It was 1973, the first year Rutgers let women enroll, and it felt like a bad omen that I was assigned a dormitory room on an all-male floor when girls had always been my allies.

On my last night home, I drove to HoJo's in Union to bid farewell to gay life. But when I went to the bathroom, there was a provocative bit of graffiti on a wall from a "houseboy" with a phone number. I felt compelled to write it down. "Houseboy" sounded young and erotic. I tucked it deep inside my wallet, for what I didn't know.

The ride from home to Rutgers took only forty minutes, but as my Dad and I unloaded the car, the distance I felt couldn't be measured in miles or minutes. I loved having a dormitory room on the top floor of a high-rise, but everything else about my new life was a scary unknown. My roommate Alan was there when we arrived. Our mothers were happy to discover we were all Jews, but that bond was soon shaken when I returned from the car with a gigantic color TV, Aunt Stella's high school graduation gift.

"What is that for?" Alan's mother asked with disdain.

"My son loves writing about entertainment and I'm all for it," my mother retorted.

As they got in the car to leave, I kissed my mom good-bye and went to hug my dad, unable to hide the apprehension in my eyes.

"Don't worry, Richie," my dad said softly. "Just be yourself and you'll be fine."

As they drove off, his words reverberated. No, I thought, one thing you don't want is for me to be myself. As I headed back upstairs, I finally felt grateful to my mother for her years of butch-up boot camp that followed her meeting with my principal when I was in third grade. The time had come to change inside.

"What are you dead? Wake up! The fire alarm went off," Alan shouted.

I couldn't make sense of the pandemonium, the deafening clanging, or the people racing past our door. Still half asleep, I shuffled to my dresser like a zombie and brushed my hair down.

"I can't believe you!" Alan said, running out the door. "The building could be burning down and you're fixing your hair!"

Now I was awake—from the sting of those words at two A.M. When I got downstairs, Alan was telling some guys about what he'd seen me do. The more they laughed, the more Alan's audience grew. It was just a fire drill, but as I wandered away from my fellow Hardenbergh Hall residents, I would have preferred a four-alarm fire to returning to my life inside.

My vow to stop being gay wasn't going well: I didn't know how. Surrounded by my peers, I felt totally alone. It was like living in gym class around the clock. I dreaded that ubiquitous conversation icebreaker, "Dja catch dat game last night?" My stomach twisted into knots each time I heard that testosterone-laden phrase: I didn't know what sport they were referring to, let alone what game. Each day was a collection of agonies that left me feeling more hopelessly queer. I made sure no one got close to me.

By the first weekend, I yearned for escape, but to where? I dug that little piece of paper out of my wallet and went to the phone booth at the end of my hall.

"Are you the houseboy?"

"No, this is Stan, my houseboy went back to college. Who's this?"

"Richard. I just started school at Rutgers and I have to get away from my dorm."

"You're eighteen?"

"I will be next month."

"Gee guy, you sound desperate to get out of there. Do you want to come here?"

I covered the mouthpiece to fight back unexpected tears. After a year at HoJo's it got so easy to pull out my dick, but I was not going to expose my emotions to a fag.

"I can pick you up at the train. I have a house deep in the woods and a built-in swimming pool. It's so secluded swimsuits are optional. It's gorgeous here at night and the forecast for the weekend is hot. Oh, wait, stop—first tell me what you look like."

On the train, I envisioned tabloid headlines. "Freshman found murdered in homo house of horror." I left Stan's phone number taped to my desk. I knew it would be found too late, but after three days of dorm life, I felt like a dead man, anyway. The question no longer was "How do I change?" but "Can I really change?" This was the year, 1973, that the American Psychiatric Association removed homosexuality from its list of mental disorders, but no one I knew cared. After my bout with crabs, my mother left newspaper clippings on my desk touting a "Clockwork Orange" cure for gay men. Patients had their eyelids taped open and were shown homoerotic images; when they became aroused, "painful stimuli were applied" in an attempt to rewire the brain so that homosexual desire would be experienced with aversion. Where religion and society had failed, science would clean up the escapees. They could have just sent them to live with my mother.

This was a good time to risk being murdered; my family would be spared the shame and I, a lifetime of pain from inflicting it. All the years of wanting to extinguish my gay desires, all the broken promises to masturbate while looking at a picture of a woman and all the effort to keep my sexuality a secret had somehow transmogrified my sexual desires into a full-fledged obsession. I got into Stan's car wondering if he'd blow me or bury me in a shallow grave in the woods.

Stan was likable and sensitive to my plight in the dorm, but I knew if I was unattractive that he would have left my pain and me at the station. I stayed all weekend. He invited friends to come by, partly to show me off, partly to provide me with a welcoming committee to the wonderful world of gay men. But each time I felt admiration for one of them while listening to their stories, a voice inside me asked, "How can you be happy when our country hates you and you're breaking your families' hearts?" When the warm, cuddly glow of Stan's vodka kicked in, I thought, oh baby, this is how.

But neither Stan nor his friends nor the high from vodka convinced me I was gay; a magazine did. When Stan fell asleep, I went hunting in search of porn. I found a treasure trove of images I'd longed for since puberty in a huge pile of soft-core magazines aptly named *After Dark*. I poured over every page of every issue completely spellbound. As I closed the cover on the last copy it was dawn in more ways than one. I knew now the only thing that would ever end my attraction to men was death. Bathroom stall graffiti had led me to a man who never said no whenever I needed refuge from four years at college.

Soon after, I befriended a girl from Spain who lived on the floor below me. At sixteen, Norma had broken off an engagement to one of the richest men in her country. Outraged, her mother imprisoned her inside their home, but Norma devised a plan of escape, pawning some of her mother's jewelry to pay for a flight to America, where a family she met agreed to take her in. I was in awe of such courage; I had a gnawing sense that I'd soon be in need of it.

A guy in our dorm pretended he liked her, but when she realized he was only using her for help in a Spanish course, she felt humiliated. I stayed up all night reminding her of how extraordinary she was. By the time the sun came up, she was over the pain and I had my first lifelong sister. Her roommate Roz talked freely about her gay brother who spent summers with his lover on Fire Island. I found a safe place with them. We became so close they began introducing me as their roommate.

One night I was carrying my pillow and blanket downstairs for a sleepover at Roz and Norma's. As I passed the guys in the lounge, they asked where I was going. When I told them they broke out into cheers, assuming I was "banging" Norma. I wanted them to just leave me alone, but they were making me the center of attention around sex.

The next day, two of them—Dan and his best friend Artie—confronted me in the hallway.

"All the guys think you're bangin' Norma, but I think you're just sleeping there, you know, like a slumber party," Dan said with a nervous twitch in his sneer.

"Yeah, a girls' slumber party," Artie chimed in.

I wouldn't lie and hurt Norma. "That's right, we're just good friends." As I masked my panic of what they'd say next, I jumped for my life on the offensive.

"You guys sit around the lounge all night talking about what girls you like, what girls you want to bed and it's all talk, talk, talk. If you ever found the balls to talk to a woman the way you talk to each other there'd be a lot more action and a lot less gab. A guy and a girl can be friends. You should try it sometime instead of feeling threatened or left out and running around casting aspersions."

As I turned to walk away, stunned by the bold choice of words that adrenaline had produced in my brain, Dan and Artie melted into competing apologies. What I said was true but it was a cover-up of precisely what they suspected. I looked away from them wondering how long I could keep up this act. This incident made them feel closer to me while I became a fraud. No wonder so many gays are actors; their life is an improvisation acted live on stage.

Rutgers had an impressive daily newspaper, *The Targum*, written and run entirely by students. A four-page centerfold devoted to the arts ran on Wednesdays. When I read that the reclusive Katharine Hepburn was doing a one-hour TV interview with Dick

Cavett, I raced to the office to see if the editors would let me review it.

The receptionist was a six-foot-tall blond woman named Trish. As I explained why I was there, I looked down and saw the book she'd been reading: *Lesbian Nation*. I'd read about that in the *Village Voice*, columnist Jill Johnston's new book about radical lesbian feminism. But this wasn't Greenwich Village. How could she sit there reading that when everyone could see the title from clear across the room? I could feel my cheeks flushing red as she pointed me toward the Arts Editor, a bearded hippie wearing a girl's pink halter top with spaghetti bows on each hairy bare shoulder. I did my best to pretend I didn't notice his outfit or the sweat dripping down my crimson cheeks.

"If you want to write TV or film reviews, the person to speak with is Walter."

He looked up as he heard his name and focused on me with a gaze so piercing, I felt he was looking right through me. Walter was wearing a Bette Midler T-shirt, a silvery glitter belt, and platform disco shoes. I looked around the office to see if anyone looked straight. They all did—except for the people I was here to see.

"Is that make-up you're wearing?" Walter had the gall to ask me.

"Of course not! My cheeks turn red when I'm perspiring or hot."

"Well tell your cheeks the air conditioning is running just fine in here."

I loathed people like him, who see someone is uncomfortable and, instead of trying to put them at ease, highlight the discomfort like a fluorescent pen.

"What can I help you with, dear?"

"The name's Richard."

"What can I help you with, Dick?"

I wanted to leave, but I was on a mission even he couldn't dissuade. "Dick Cavett is doing an unprecedented one-hour interview with—"

"The calla lilies are in bloom again," Walter said, shaking all over in a demeaning impersonation of the elderly Hepburn. "Sure, you can review it, just keep it under a thousand words and get it in here fast so it's timely. Leave me your phone number so I can, uh, reach you for editing."

As I walked back to my room, my head was spinning. When I stepped off the elevator, I heard, "Berkowitz, phone call, Walter. Tell that guy to wait a minute between tries; some of us are actually trying to study."

Over the course of the following month, Walter and I locked horns constantly. He was determined to yank me out of the closet while I was equally determined to stay in. And in that battle, he made my life a living hell. Every time Walter saw me eating at the Commons with Dan and Artie or with Roz and Norma, he would drag members of the Homophile League by our table, pointing me out to them in his Carmen Miranda or Judy Garland T-shirt. I begged him from the phone booth to stop calling me ten times a day because the guys on my floor were annoyed and getting suspicious. I pleaded with him to consider the consequences if my floor mates thought they were living with a queer, but to no avail.

"You can't run away from who you are," Walter proclaimed. "I know. I tried."

"You presumptuous prick—you don't know shit about me."

"I know straight guys don't have 'Kate on Cavett' marked on their calendars."

As I came out of the phone booth exasperated, Dan and Artie were standing at the end of the hall in a confrontational stance.

"That guy Walter who keeps calling you, isn't he that flaming fag from the *Targum?*" asked Dan.

"He's just my editor and I know what you're thinking but—"

"No! Don't *you* tell us what to think again. You don't take calls from a fag night and day unless you're a fag, too. I can understand you lyin', 'cause it shows that even though you're a low-life cock-sucking faggot, you have enough sense to try and hide it."

I fled to my room like a cornered rat. I didn't even check which guys were around us watching. It doesn't matter, they'll all know soon. Alan could walk in and I won't even have a corner of privacy to hide in. Wait till he finds out his roommate's a fag. My existence is contaminating. I could kill Walter. Gay men, straight men, they all make me wanna puke.

Word got out. Some guys on my floor kicked and spat on my door when they walked past. I stopped taking the dorm elevator and used the stairs, which ended my happiness living atop a high-rise. I was afraid of being ambushed and beaten. I was having trouble digesting food and had constant stomach pains. I went home to see an internist who stuck a thick metal tube up my rectum to examine me inside. It felt like a minute of being raped. It was the final humiliation; like a switch had been flipped, my whole being went numb and stayed that way.

Coming up the stairs after a day of classes, as I was about to open the door to my floor, I heard my name; guys in the lounge were talking about me being a fag. I froze at the sound of laughter. I didn't know what to do or where to turn so I kept going up and discovered an entry to the roof. I stepped out and began walking toward the edge trying to muster the will to just keep walking. But the closer I got, the more terrified I became and I couldn't shake the thought that the reason I wanted to do this was the reason I couldn't do this, because I was a weak pathetic fag in a world where you can never be butch enough. Maybe I could lie down, close my eyes, and just keep rolling around until I eventually went over the edge; this way I could avoid that moment of terror and decision until I finally fell free. I couldn't go back down there. Any more than I could do this.

If only I could have known that Dan would walk up to me in a gay bar after his own decade-long struggle to come out. Or that it was her own tortured lesbianism before she came out of the closet that led my third-grade teacher to turn an eight-year-old's birthday party into a scandal. If I had, that desperate, lonely moment on a dormitory rooftop wouldn't have occurred. But it did.

I leaned back on a retainer wall and sunk to the ground while the sun began to set. As I took in a panoramic view of the gorgeous autumnal campus, I became fixated on the block known as "the wall." It was a place I'd heard about where frat guys went to beat up gay men who went there late at night to cruise. It was completely crazy, but some force inside me—loneliness? horniness? insanity?—compelled me to go. I watched and waited for the sky to become night. Then I went downstairs, put on my baseball jacket and headed to the wall in the cover of darkness with a gut full of fear, rage, and burning sexual desire. But at least I no longer felt numb.

To my chagrin, the only men there were much older, not students as I had expected. I was the only one not cruising in a car, making me an easy target for attack. The longer I stayed the more I feared being assaulted, but it didn't diminish my reckless determination to find sex, it just fueled a greater urgency to find it. Pleasure and danger—why was that all gay life was?

As car after car slowed down to a crawl when they passed me, I recalled an incident at HoJo's. A man had pulled his car up next to mine and kept waving a fan of $20 bills at me. I was horny, he was decent looking, so I let him blow me and fifteen minutes later I had $80. Could that be a way to afford a room away from my dorm? There was only one way to find out.

Another man slowed his car as he passed, then pulled over and shut his headlights. While talking to him in his car, he seemed desperate to have sex with me. I learned from my months at HoJo's that the more masculine I acted, the more desirable gay men found me. It was time to take that act to another level.

"I really would like to go with you, but I just stopped by to look for a guy I met here before. I'm so fucking horny," I said, rubbing my palm across my crotch, "but I need to see if this guy shows up because, well . . . don't be offended by this—I really do like the guy—but he gives me money anyway just to service me. Being in school full time, it really helps. I'm certainly not expecting you to do that and if he doesn't show up maybe I'll see you later, but don't wait for me."

As I moved to get out of his car, he made me an offer I didn't refuse. Twenty minutes later he thanked me and dropped me off. I couldn't believe how detached and cool I felt. Those men at the wall were looking for the all-American college jock and the way they gawked at me, in my little baseball jacket, left me thinking I could fulfill that fantasy. They had no idea the jacket was the only thing I didn't hate about baseball. At my dorm, faggots were the lowest forms of life, but on a remote dark corner of campus, I wasn't just worshipped, I got paid. It was time to alter my vow: I wouldn't give up trying not to waste my life being gay, but I could exploit it for the money and blow jobs, which as far as I could see, was all gay life had to offer anyway. Getting paid was proof that I was too good for gay life. There had to be some way to rise above it.

The next night I returned I struck up a conversation with a flamboyant black man named Cecile. I felt safer talking to someone while I was there but I ended up pouring out all my problems at the dorm. When I finally shut up, Cecile led me around the block to a submarine sandwich shop he owned named My Hero. He warned me of the dangers at the wall—muggers, gay-bashers, police harassment, and drunken frat guys who lived a block away. Then he offered me a job, a bit under minimum wage but with free food. I grabbed it. I now had a safe haven from the cafeteria, a place to digest a meal.

Prostitute? What the hell was I thinking?

By late October I had perfected a new skill, how to live in close quarters without ever acknowledging the people around you are there. I could finally start concentrating on my major, Communications. The department had overhauled the curriculum with a radical new approach based on teaching theory. The first required reading was a skimpy little book that would mark a revolution in my thinking, or the beginning of it, *The Social Construction of Reality: A Treatise in the Sociology of Knowledge,* by Peter Berger and Thomas Luckmann. Could reality be socially constructed, and if it was man-made, why couldn't it be person-changed? I thought of the American Psychiatric Association, waving its magic wand of power and poof: millions of people were instantly transformed from sick to well. It started me down a path of questioning what I accepted as truth, what I accepted as reality, what I accepted as normal. Prodded by this and similar books that dissected the world through social psychology, I started thinking for myself and seeing the world around me as if for the first time. These books kept using examples of racism and sexism to illustrate their theories that the rules and values of any given society are fluid and changing, but they could have just as easily used homophobia to illustrate many of the same points. Not that I needed them to, that was my homework and my professors loved what was I was doing, taking class lectures on theories and applying them in my everyday world. I took my first steps out of the closet by challenging my own professors to live up to the lessons they were teaching. None disappointed me; all respected my privacy. The more I learned in class, the more I realized my days in the closet were numbered. My textbooks contained all the arguments anyone could need to conduct a successful revolution for cocksuckers and other assorted outcasts and perverts of the day.

⇐　⇒

While at home on spring break, I went to HoJo's, right near home in Union. I wanted to challenge the fears that constricted me, and I was about to be put to the test.

As I came out of the restaurant one night, a girl was screaming my name, and not just my first name, my whole name. She was skipping and jumping as she raced toward me and her gigantic breasts were bouncing up and down and all over the place in a low-cut, 1940s gold lamé gown. She was wearing yellow, six-inch high heels, and a huge black feather boa. Who the hell was this and why did she have to be so loud?

"Remember me? Barbara Serle, though now I'm just known as Babs, Babs Divine. We sang together in Beth Shalom choir. I was at Union High School last year when you graduated. Oh honey, I knew your story all along with those red, rosy cheeks, and it's so fabulous that you finally figured it out too—and in time to still be chicken!"

"Figured what out?"

"Oh puh-leeze Louise, don't be a tired closet queen. You'll never convince these tits you're at HoJo's after midnight for the fried clams so just get over it *right now!*"

She pulled me to her car where she blasted the radio and began disco dancing lewdly around the lot, shaking her enormous breasts, thrusting her hips, and flinging her boa like a star onstage. She was so outrageous and obscene, I couldn't stop laughing at the horrified reactions of weary Parkway motorists who had stopped for a meal and ended up with a bawdy floorshow. Everyone watching her was appalled, but she just soaked in their attention, stuck out her chest at them and belted out a perverted version of Bob Hope's theme song, "Thanks for the Mammaries."

As I caught myself in a fit of uncontrollable laughter out in the open—in the middle of the faygala-infested area of the parking lot—being hugged, groped, and celebrated for who I really was, I could finally taste what it felt like to be free. Barbara grabbed a camera out of her car and took pictures of me laughing hysterically. As the flashes went off and lit up the night, a bunch of cars tore out of the gay section of the lot.

"That's the problem with these faygalas—no one wants to come out, they just want to come. I think we wreaked enough havoc here so get your buns in my car. I'm taking you to the most fabulous gay disco Manhattan has ever seen, Le Jardin." She was like all the Marx Brothers rolled into one. I jumped in on my way to my first gay bar.

The club was elegant and the people looked so chic I couldn't believe the place was gay. As we made our way through the crowd, gorgeous men were dancing with each other under bright spotlights as if nothing was wrong with it. I needed a moment to adapt, but Barbara dragged me to the center of the dancing crowd. When Bette Midler's "Boogie Woogie Bugle Boy" began playing, she went wild, shimmying her breasts all around the dance floor, which cleared to watch and applaud her. One guy grabbed her thinking she was Bette Midler.

"Honey, that bitch stole my act!" Gay men all around us roared with laughter.

She took me to gay places during the day, in the sunshine, shops along Christopher Street, gay restaurants in Greenwich Village, and everywhere we went was a stage for her campy theatrics. She told me painful stories of how she was humiliated and harassed when she hit puberty and developed into a 38 triple D bra size while standing only 5' 1". After bouts with suicidal feelings, one day she shoved her breasts in the embarrassed face of one of tormentors and decided to boldly be herself and to hell with what people said or thought.

She taught me how a social outcast becomes a survivor by learning to love yourself. She was my salvation, my second lifelong sister. It took a seventeen-year-old feminist to show me that gay life could be more than sex in the dark with strangers. With her, I began meeting gay people away from seedy cruising spots. My aching for sex was expanding into an aching for love. If only I had a clue of how damaged I already was and of the damage yet to come.

"Berkowitz, phone call, Walter. Why don't you two move in to-gether and give us a break?"

"What's up, glamour girl?"

"Get over here to *Targum* right now! Dean Crosby was gay-bashed last night."

"The dean of students?"

"*Yes!* I've only told you about him a dozen times but it's a measure of how well you've adapted to gay male life that anyone who isn't drop-dead gorgeous is so difficult to keep track of."

"Why are you being so vicious?"

"I call it like I see it, whatever's left standing is fine with me. He's in bad shape—head trauma. They haven't decided who's writ-ing the story—"

"But it'll be a whitewash."

"Hello! You want to be a writer? Write something. Go talk to him."

But I didn't want to see him or anyone like that. It felt ghoulish to go there to invade his privacy in order to exploit an act of vio-lence for a cause. As I imagined that frail, gentle man in his 50s lying in the infirmary battered and bloodied, I felt sick that it could one day be me, and enraged it had happened to him. It seemed like every step I took forward in my self-esteem as a gay man increased my anger at the hostile world around me. I adapted to living in a protective cocoon of my own hostility, but if a dean of students could end up beaten to a pulp, any of us could. I thought coming out in the '70s would be a continual march forward into a brighter day, but it was getting darker before we'd ever see that dawn. Maybe Walter had a point. Gorgeous guys were the balm for the disap-pointments in the struggle. Or did he mean they were replacing it?

"Berkowitz, phone, who else?"

"What's up Ernestine?"

"Phoenicia, listen to the ad the Homophile League just brought in for tomorrow's edition of the *Targum*. 'National Gay Day or how to turn your dungarees into hot pants. On Friday a census will be taken of all gay people on the Rutgers Campus. To make it easier to see who's straight and who's gay, anyone wearing blue jeans will be registered as gay. If you're NOT gay, and all you got is blue jeans, get back in the closet and keep looking honey!'"

As the League well knew, in 1974, most students owned nothing but blue jeans. Furious complaints could be heard in the cafeteria and dorm lounges and as Friday drew near students panicked. But for those who understood the joke, that it was just a way to get people to think about an issue most people were too afraid even to discuss, it was a moment of inspiration with a touch of humor.

But the following year, when the League ran a similar ad, the humor died. The Delta Kappa Epsilon (DKE) fraternity, known as the frat for jocks, hung an effigy with a rope around its neck from a tree in front of their house on College Avenue. It wore a sign that read, "The only good gay is a dead gay. Back to your closets homos." To underscore their lynching theme, a pool stick was impaled through the effigy's chest.

As I stood underneath it, stunned in disbelief at the lifeless figure swaying in the breeze, students kept passing, a few registering disgust, sizing up the house of frat jocks, and moving on. No one had the courage to confront them except the three lesbians parked on the frat stoop who looked like they were in no hurry to leave and too outraged to be afraid. They had more courage than I did. I ran to the *Targum* office to get a reporter, but no one would cover it. I could grab my shoulder bag and get Walter in his platform disco shoes and go join the lesbians on the porch, or I could throw myself at a typewriter and fight the best way I knew how.

A biting editorial spewed out of me while Trish and Walter cheered me on. As I constructed each sentence to publicly humiliate a house full of frat jocks, I worried that I was being irrational; no one ever defended gays and by doing so I would officially and publicly declare myself as one in 16,000 copies of the next day's *Targum*, with no way to run a retraction, no going back. Having finally been able to afford moving out of the dorm where I felt a vague threat of danger fueled by the hallway humiliation from Dan, I thought I was safe. But I'd planted myself in a rooming house half a block behind DKE, which I now knew with certainty wasn't just a clear threat of danger but a proud, arrogant symbol of it, a chilling fact of life, something I had to face. I could water down what I was writing, but I couldn't walk away. Anger had become my constant companion; it wouldn't let me stay silent anymore.

My column sparked a huge response at the *Targum* office, generating more letters to the editor over an issue than I'd ever seen, and they appeared all week. Most attacked DKE, but not all, especially the longest ones from defensive DKE brothers themselves. Walter renamed me Polly Political, a moniker that stuck for years. Homophile League President Kevin Vericker came to the office and told me that we had to exploit the response to my editorial by organizing a protest. I called the *Village Voice*'s gay columnist, Arthur Bell, and convinced him to come speak. The National Organization for Women referred me to lesbian activist Kay Whitlock, who joined Bell.

When hundreds showed up at the rally and marched to the frat house, I broke out laughing at the thought of my mother seeing what her son was accomplishing in college. I had sparked New Jersey's first gay rights demonstration. It was a moment to take stock of the journey here. And at the annual shirt-and-tie *Targum* banquet the next month, I watched in awe as Walter brought the festivities to a momentary, disquieting halt when he walked in chillingly dressed as the effigy, a far cry from our usual outlandish attire as the gays who ruled the critiques staff. That's what gay liberation was in the '70s, ordinary people doing courageous things that would never be recorded by history or promoted by publicists for self-promotion and personal gain.

Later that year, my dad called to say he needed to use my college loan money to pay the mortgage on our house. After working hard all his life as a manual laborer, it was devastating to hear my father sound ashamed and dispirited. I couldn't stand not acknowledging how awful he sounded, but I couldn't find the right words to say. I left My Hero for a better-paying job at a convenience store, hoping to send him some money, but time doesn't wait for minimum wage earners. The day before my first paycheck came, my father died.

I'd never know what he thought of the person that I turned out to be, and now that he was gone, what I turned out to be felt eerily less important. When we got home from the cemetery, my mother guided her rabbi over to me to pose a question to him that was obviously going to be for my benefit. "What does Judaism advise a mother to do if he she has a homosexual son?"

Munching on something, he looked up at her long enough to glibly reply, "Recite Yizkor for one year," and resumed chewing, oblivious to the violent bite with which he had just ripped a chunk out of me.

Yizkor is the Jewish prayer for the dead. On the day I buried my father, my faith buried me.

When the fog of grief lifted, the sun came back out and confirmed my suspicions: the world was depleted. I couldn't see much left that warranted the level of respect my dad had inspired with a depth I couldn't fully fathom until he was suddenly gone.

That summer when my mother needed me most, I felt I couldn't go home anymore. I was now my only home. That was a scary realization, but I latched onto the first bright side I could find: My sexuality felt freed from all constraints. And from God, too. A forty-minute train ride to Manhattan was all it took to go from my room to a hot, sweaty night in one of New York City's dozen gay bathhouses, my new houses of worship that welcomed me with open arms.

In between the train station and my boarding house was the wall. Even in a little town like New Brunswick, gay men were starting to claim this block as their public space. It was in the way they were coming out of their cars, cruising in pairs and hanging out in boisterous cliques, watching each other's backs instead of looking over a lonely shoulder. I dated and had a few affairs and got to know some of the local gay men. Making the most of my time hanging out there, I also found several men who were eager to come to my rented room a block away and discreetly blow me for bucks. It took four or five return visits before it sunk into my brain that each of these guys were becoming a regular part of my life. I was freed from the minimalist earnings of convenience chain store employment.

I knew I could hustle at the wall, but it wasn't until after my father died that I felt I could do it without caring what anyone thought. I never felt my self-esteem was on the line, and I liked the sense of danger, the acting, and the practicality. If I was going to spend time cruising, I wanted a cute guy, but I'd just turned twenty and the average age at cruise areas was forty . . . so it was like, if you're gonna keep flirting and chatting with me all night while I look for someone cute, I may as well take advantage of how frustrated we've gotten when I'm ready to call it a night and we're both horny. I had no idea that a handful of guys I took back to my room for pocket money that summer would keep coming back and end my need for a part-time job until I graduated Rutgers. In fact, it was unsettling to realize that my half-dozen improvisations as a hustler ended up making me one. But then I recalled the dairy case stench when I restocked milk cartons at Krauszers, and I did a little dance.

My savings account was growing fast. It made me feel self-sufficient, but not happy. In fact, it underscored a lingering sadness: I could have paid the mortgage with ease. My father believed that men should be the breadwinners, he believed in honest hard work and the American way. I believed it wore him out, drowned him in debt, left him feeling he had failed as a man, and sent him to a premature grave at fifty-four. At twenty, I was set on doing things my own way.

1976 was America's Bicentennial, but after Watergate, Vietnam, recessions, and the assassinations of two Kennedys and Martin Luther King, few seemed motivated to celebrate. The volatile political activism that erupted on many American college campuses in the late 1960s had given way to cynicism and apathy in the 1970s. There were three exceptions, feminists, blacks, and gays, but overall the passions of the 1960s seemed to have faded along with the sheer numbers of people actively getting involved. Those of us who did never seemed to seize the one chance that we had: to join forces and build coalitions that could have made us a force to be reckoned with. We couldn't seem to talk past the barriers—of race and sex and sexual orientation—that separated us.

But at each annual Gay Pride march in New York City, the mood was like a street party as queers took over the streets like inmates suddenly running the asylum. Activists from every left-wing cause descended on our huge parade, trying to get gays to join their struggles. There were radical socialists, abortion rights activists, prison reformers, women's health care collectives, anarchists, environmentalists, critics of the military industrial complex, workers' rights advocates, and coalitions fighting to end third world poverty. It inspired me to see so many groups that were able to keep going and were trying to make the world better. And it felt good to see that some people wanted us; no one else did.

Growing up in a family of northeastern liberal Jewish Democrats, surrounded by lively discussions that were empathetic on social issues while debating controversies that kept popping out of the late 1960s, provided fertile ground for the impact that lesbian and gay liberation in the 1970s had on me. Each year on the last Sunday in June, Babs and I made our way to Gay Pride Day in New York City. I soaked in sights, slogans, and a sea of people that would be my source of inspiration in moments when I felt self-doubt, isolated, or hopeless about America ever feeling like home to me again. Whether it was the moving sight of a "Grandma for gays" or the way ordinary people used the march down Fifth Avenue to respond with humor to the latest media attack ("Nobody ever recruited me, I enlisted on my own!"), it was spiritual fuel to take back home for the struggle to heal my own sense of stigma about being gay. Activism was my expression of gratitude for being a survivor, one young gay man who didn't end up leaping off a rooftop; it was also to take a stand for those who did and those who were pushed, tallied in tiny, one-paragraph articles, scattered on the pages of a burgeoning gay press. I had to say thanks to a movement that let me know I was not alone. That's how I'd been raised.

Being gay was only a part of me, but it was the only part of me that had ever felt like it could have killed me, so I embraced it as who I was, my emotional identity, my new religion. In 1977, the year I was graduating from Rutgers, Walter organized a university forum, "The Changing Stereotypes of Women, Blacks and Gays in Film," and put me on the panel. I came across a nationally syndicated advice column by Ann Landers, in which a man wrote to object that she called gays "sick." Landers, who'd been dubbed "the most influential woman in America," replied, "I do NOT believe homosexuality is 'just another lifestyle.' I believe these people suffer from a severe personality disorder. Granted, some are sicker than others, but sick they are, and all the fancy rhetoric by the American Psychiatric Association will not change it."

At the forum, I began by reading her letter and then my reply to her reply.

> Dear Ann Landers,
>
> Have you taken a look lately at the heartbreaking statistics of rape and wife battering? Are you aware that heterosexual men perpetrate the vast majority of child abuse cases in the country? Half of all marriages now end in divorce, which includes your own recently defunct matrimony. Who can assume the 50% that remain are happy and healthy? In view of all this violence and human misery, I do not believe heterosexuality is "just another lifestyle." Granted, some of these heteros are sicker than others, but sick they are, and all your fancy rhetoric won't obscure the fact that the leading cause of violence against American females is heterosexual men.

I looked out into the audience with feigned innocence. "I just wanted to turn the table to show how it feels from the other side. I long for the day when public figures like Landers feel as uncomfortable espousing gross generalizations about gay people as I just did about straights." But inside I was snickering; I had just put down heterosexuals to their faces under the ruse of illustrating a point and received considerable applause. My anger was turning into arrogance, but I didn't realize that was a signal for stupidity and a symptom of something missing between the back-and-forth rut of angry politics and bathhouse bliss—feeling unloved and fearing I always would be.

By senior year, my visibility on campus as Targum's gay writer made me a mother hen to a small flock of students who were as tormented as I once was about being gay. I wanted to do for them what Barbara did for me—help them accept who they were. Two twin brothers, who discovered they were both gay by separately befriending me, said they had a bisexual friend who wanted a date with me.

"Bisexuals are fence-sitting queers who don't have the guts to be gay," I said in my smug activist mode. "I'm not interested in dating half of someone's sexuality."

"Rob is gorgeous," the twins announced in stereo. The plan was to meet at Kirkpatrick Chapel for a Christmas carol concert given by the Rutgers choir composed almost entirely of gay men.

This was too perverse to pass up, a radical queer Jew-turned-atheist on a gay blind date in a church.

Gorgeous was not the word. Rob looked like the answer to my dreams. He had soft, angelic ringlets for hair, a compact, perfect body, and a cocky, streetwise manner that came from growing up poor in the city. I couldn't believe he wanted me. I felt good-looking, but by the increasingly brutal standards of urban gay male life, I wasn't in his league. Luckily, a clueless bisexual wouldn't be aware of that. Or could I be fortunate enough to be desired by someone who valued something more?

A friend had given me a joint I had never known what to do with until now. When the concert finally ended, I asked Rob, "Want to come to my room and smoke a joint?"

"Sure," Rob said as his face lit up. I practically swooned.

As we walked to my place, I worried that I should have been more sociable and asked him out for a drink. But I knew he wanted me—he had set up the date—and I wanted him more than anyone I'd ever seen. He was so smart, and I felt such immediate happiness just being with him, it was as if the whole tortured journey to coming out was nothing if I could just cradle him in my arms. For so many years I reined in my feelings and hid my desires and I was lonely and worried that I'd never find love. And here was this beautiful guy staring at me with this I'm-all-yours look in his eyes, who had the courage to take a chance, to be vulnerable and risk rejection in front of friends, to reach out to me. When we got to my room, I put Donna Summer's "Could This Be Magic?" on the stereo. It was an innocuous song but there was a longing for passion in Summer's voice that transcended the material and connected me so powerfully with my deepest yearning for someone to love. I knew this could be that moment I'd longed for as I turned from the stereo and saw Rob sitting on my bed, kicking off his shoes.

Several puffs into the joint I scooped him up into my arms and I lost myself in kissing him. I rolled him onto his stomach and as I slid off his jeans, I beheld the most beautiful dimpled butt I had ever seen. Without meaning to, I blurted out, "Oh my God."

"What's wrong?" Rob asked in a panic.

I couldn't think of anything to say but the truth—a radical concept since growing up gay had trained me to be an adept liar probably even in my sleep. But I also didn't want to lie—I was craving intimacy, and I had no idea why I suddenly knew that it only comes from honesty and trust. I could only guess it came from my father, but seeing Rob and me like this could have done him in.

"Nothing is wrong. I just never understood the desire to fuck a man's butt until now."

The reassuring look in Rob's eyes was all the reward I needed for my vulnerable admission that in spite of all my know-it-all arrogance, I had never even experienced intercourse. I was a slut and a whore, but technically speaking, I was still a virgin and not just to intercourse but to sex with the whole person, the body and the soul, the person and his history. The connection I felt to Rob tugged at my heart and my dick and introduced them to each other as if for the first time, as I began to make love so sweet and tender and passionate I didn't know where inside me it came from. I felt driven by a powerful need to be inside him in whatever way I could. I didn't know what I was doing when I entered him, but waves of ecstasy seemed to rush through our bodies and came pouring out of our eyes as the subtlest movement of my hips registered the most intense emotions and joy in Rob's face—emotions that I missed with oral sex, which was disconnected. Crotch to face, instead of face to face, was the only sex I had known. For a moment I thought I was dripping sweat on him, but the window next to the bed was open and snowflakes were blowing in. Losing myself inside him, in this strange, extraordinary communion of our bodies, locked into each other's eyes and arms, it was as if the two of us were melting into one. Not since I was a singing, dancing kid had I felt such perfect happiness in my own skin and I realized it wasn't sweat dripping. That twinkle in Rob's eyes was from seeing tears fall from mine. I felt so emotionally naked and exposed, my instinct was to run and hide, but the look on Rob's face seemed to say, you're safe, we're home. All the things we were taught that men weren't supposed to be with each other, weepy, tender, emotional, soft, sensual, sexual, vulnerable, we could be with each other.

There was no Kabuki dance around who would make the next move or call. It felt like a miracle we had found each other. After years of reining in feelings and hiding desires, conditioned with precision to be able to recognize that moment, that second, when a look exchanged between men goes from casual to threatening to an invitation to a violent threat, Rob and I awoke the next morning and knew: becoming instantly inseparable was freedom. I changed my phone number to cut out hustling and told Rob all about it. I longed for a place without secrets.

Every night we'd crawl into bed like two happy little kids and wrap our bodies around each other to sleep. It felt like peace on earth, a feeling of overwhelming calm, connection, and joy that I never felt before. Nothing compares to the feeling of falling in love. After graduation, we stayed put, shut off from the world in our romance.

But again, fall ushered in a chill that changed everything. I was accepted into New York University graduate film school, but every clinical psychology program he applied to had rejected Rob. With our lives about to go off in opposite directions, we moved to an apartment a mile from the Lincoln Tunnel in Hudson County, New Jersey, where Rob had grown up and his family lived. It was practical, affordable, and the biggest mistake we made.

"Now we have to be discreet," Rob sadly warned. We had to stay on guard when we were in public to make sure we didn't look like we were in love. We had to keep a second bed in our tiny apartment to hide that we slept together. Whenever a family member called to stop by, we raced around the apartment to make sure gay newspapers and magazines were hidden. The fearlessness we took for granted at college was fading into cowardice. I became consumed with bouts of insecurity. Was it being gay that he was hiding—or loving me?

My contempt for hiding revived the anger that love had soothed.

Rob began drinking while I was away all day at school, and tension between us mounted as film shoots lengthened a full day of classes and I had to add a part-time job. Every night as I hurried through Greenwich Village to get the subway and bus home, I saw gay life bursting out of the bars and pouring into the streets. Gay men were creating a radical new subculture of sex and pleasure— without the danger or furtiveness. There was safety in numbers and a profoundly moving visibility that could only blossom ghettoized away from the suffocating pressures of family and society. New gay bars, discos, and sex clubs were opening every month. The billboard on Christopher Street over Sheridan Square brazenly advertised a hot, new bathhouse called Man's Country. Guys tried to pick me up on the street and in the subway. It was getting hard to go home to Rob fussing over keeping my dinner warm while gay and sexual freedom was on fire in the city. I hated myself for wanting it, and I hated knowing that no matter how fast I rushed home, it was never early enough for Rob.

How did we end up like a second-rate married couple, like heteros but in hiding? Here I was at twenty-three and in my prime, spending three hours a day commuting a couple of miles to a roach-infested apartment, in an overcrowded, suffocating town where you couldn't cross the sidewalk without stepping in dog shit. I kept thinking, We could be spending those three hours together. I have to get us out of there.

"You have some talent," my adviser warned, "but you're too distracted, racing back to Jersey every night like a husband with a wife in labor. You need to make a choice or accept your heart's not here."

She was right; my heart belonged in a world that didn't yet exist. But Greenwich Village was close enough for me. I decided: Rob either moves here with me or he can join me when he's ready.

But I couldn't afford to return for the second year of my master's program. I increased my job to full time, but I never did the math. When the following September rolled around, I still couldn't go back to school, and Rob was working in New Jersey with autistic kids but wouldn't move to Manhattan. I was granted an unusual second year's financial leave of absence, but that was all. This next year was do or die.

One night as Rob and I walked along Boulevard East overlooking its breathtaking view of the Manhattan skyline, Rob muttered, "Life is pain."

"Rob," I blurted out, "life is what you make it. Neither of us has been happy since we moved here and the dream I've been busting my ass to reach has been on hold on the other side of this river for two years." I paused as we looked across the river at my new life beckoning. Rob was silent. I took his hand and said, "You will always have a place in my life and I hope the day comes when our lives can intersect the way they did before we moved here but I can't wait anymore. I wish I could pick you up and drag you with me but I can't. I will be there for you in a second any time you need me. And for as long as I live and for as long as you want me, I'm your family as much as if we were by blood."

Life is pain. I ran from those prophetic words as fast as I could and into the center of a gathering storm.

⤺   ⤼

Finding an apartment within the bustling gay ghetto in Greenwich Village was impossible, so I settled on West 15th Street (in what would a decade later become the new gay ghetto of Chelsea). I couldn't bear thinking about the pain I had caused Rob by abandoning him, and I was terrified I'd never find love like that again. Salvaging what we could, Rob and I morphed into wounded brothers. But wounds can heal.

If working full time was just enough to live on, you guessed it, hustling was the only instant option left to get my master's degree. I visited a hustler's bar called Cowboys/Cowgirls on the Upper East Side of Manhattan and went home with a wealthy executive who turned out to be a nasty alcoholic. He paid me $150—almost a week's salary at my job—but afterwards, I felt used and hurt because for the first time someone I had had sex with for money didn't care about seeing me again or care about me at all.

A few weeks later, I saw an article in the *New York Post* (December 28, 1979, page 10) titled "Women Dinner Guests Quizzed in Killing." The executive I had gone home with had been found in his townhouse murdered, "naked and wrapped in a bloodied blanket." It was a wake-up call to forget about picking up strangers in bars and, as with most jobs, to be nice even when it wasn't deserved.

Since my one experience hustling in New York City had introduced me to the victim of a violent murder, I had to find an alternative where I could examine someone's personality and certify that they were gay (and not a killer of gays or the police) under the guise of conversation before determining whether to meet them. I could do that by phone. I decided to try a "Models/Masseurs" ad in the *Advocate,* a national gay newspaper I often read. And as preparation, I called one of the ads to ask if I needed to know how to give massages.

"Of course not," the man said, laughing. "It's just a euphemism." He sounded so happy and I was shocked that he felt free to tell a stranger what it was like running his ad. He had no paranoia, no shame, no fears, and he even offered me advice. "If you're really twenty-three, say you're eighteen or you'll make the rest of us look like liars, and if you look as hot as you sound, you'll do well."

As the weeks went by waiting for my ad to appear, I kept panicking. Manhattan wasn't suburban New Jersey; there were gorgeous gay men everywhere who were migrating here from all over the country. With all these hot guys giving sex away for free, why would anyone need to pay me?

On the day my ad appeared I was too broke for insecurities. I took a deep breath each time the phone rang and dove in. Two men wanted to come over at the same time. I saw one in the morning and pushed the other one back to the afternoon. As soon as I opened my door to let them in, both said the same thing: "You're really twenty-three!" (I had just turned twenty-four but from the reactions I got I was glad I ditched that awful advice to pretend I was eighteen.)

In a few days, men I had seen were coming back while the flow of new clients didn't let up. Manhattan was filled with successful men who didn't have time to play cat-and-mouse games in gay bars; for others, privacy was their first concern. On the phone it was apparent that I was educated, businesslike, and serious—just like majority of men calling these ads.

I realized I had struck gold and disco-danced around my apartment tossing hundred dollar bills in the air to the blasting beat of Blondie's "Call Me."

It seemed like a mystical coincidence that just as I began feeling haunted by the stigma attached to sex work that I had once felt about being gay, the movie *American Gigolo* opened in New York City. It completely glamorized hustling as only Hollywood could. After the movie, I stopped into Barney's two blocks from my apartment to shop for something by Giorgio Armani, the clothes designer for *American Gigolo*.

Browsing through the most gorgeous ties I'd ever seen I realized what was bothering me. Growing up I was taught that the worst thing you could be if you were a man was a queer, and the worst thing you could be if you were a woman was a whore. Then came my moment of epiphany: It was now my mission to have the time of my life being both. No one but my closest friends would ever know I was doing this—it's not like I'd ever write a book about it. And doing something so stigmatized, detested, and illegal, which already described my life as a gay man, also felt like a way to accord my country the same disregard it accorded me. It wasn't as if being a monogamous gay man in love was seen as any better, so fuck it, I'll be a gigolo. I took two ties to the cashier and handed the clerk a hundred-dollar bill. Good riddance to the hungry years.

I was done trying to change the world, or to fit into it, but I couldn't see how completely the world had changed me.

It was now January 1980.

2

The Big Bang

AIDS hits home

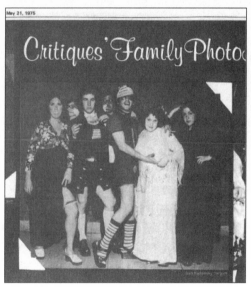

Targum's Arts staff, annual banquet 1975 (Rutgers)

Overcoming the stigma embedded in my sexual awakening as a gay teen led me to question and discard what little I was taught about sex. There were no role models to guide me, no images in popular culture that affirmed my existence, no family to embrace all of me, just a rabbi to declare me dead. The powerful sexual drive of my adolescence led me to have sex with men I didn't know and didn't want to know: I wanted to be normal, happy, and loved, not "sick" or a man "you have to feel sorry for" or "a disease." No matter how frightened I was, however, my desires kept pulling me back to men I'd been taught to pity, to a life that everyone condemned, because those desires I was fighting, *those desires were me.* At eighteen, I was finally able call a truce in the five-year war against myself; my wounds were internal, so as long as they were out of sight, they were out of mind. With my mother's determination, my father's compassion, Uncle Marvin and Aunt Stella's unconditional love, and Judaism's survival lesson to own one's difference and know who you are, I had found my way home to the celebration that had started it all, Christopher Street in Greenwich Village.

My lonely formative years before coming out served as a prep school for hustling in the fast lane of gay Manhattan. This clandestine, "immoral," illegal and widely detested activity felt like familiar terrain. After all, the list of adjectives just mentioned applied to gay sex in general when I came of age. Sexually transmitted infections (STIs) were rampant among sexually active urban gay men in 1980, so for a hustler, that was an ever-present concern. Hustling was about to give me a unique window into the most secret sexual desires of many men, desires that would soon emerge as a central issue in coping with the coming plague of AIDS.

Sex work turned my life into a mass of contradictions. I loved the fast-paced and lucrative lifestyle of an escort, but I hated getting STIs with such ferocity, and there was no way I was going to just accept them as an occupational hazard to be taken in stride.

In 1980, the sexual revolution had already reached its zenith. It was a time of blissful sexual abandon. But for me, that abandon was interrupted as soon as I encountered my first STIs. All my years of sexual activity in New Jersey had only given me a case of crabs. But during college I got stuck in Manhattan one night after missing the last bus back to school and went to stay at a gay bathhouse until morning. I had sex with one man and three days later, I was at the school infirmary with a burning case of penile gonorrhea. It was easy to figure out that in a place where people could have multiple sexual partners in a short span of time, the risk of getting infected with something was greatly increased. My initiation to bathhouse sex was my introduction to disease, propelling me on a long quest of altering my sexual behavior to avoid infections but without giving up sex, even at the baths.

"Why go back?" one might ask. Coming of age in the 1970s, many young gay men outside cities had no concept of sex *without* danger—of being found out, disgraced, arrested, beaten up, etc. STIs were just one more thing to be added to a long list.

When I came to live in New York City after my breakup with Rob, I felt like the proverbial kid in the candy store with endless opportunities for sex. The first week I went to the baths twice, but since my maiden voyage had given me penile gonorrhea I was gun-shy. The treatment for penile gonorrhea was easy—just swallow some pills. But the test for penile gonorrhea was horrible; I started to faint watching a Q-tip being pushed into the slit of my penis. So when I went to the baths the week I moved here, without knowing better, I gave oral sex but wouldn't receive it—but I still got sick by the week's end. I woke up one morning with piercing stomach cramps and diarrhea. I felt horrible, but I lived eight blocks from a gay health clinic, so I ran.

The Gay Men's Health Project faced Sheridan Square, the site of the Stonewall Bar where gay liberation began in 1969. Many doctors volunteered at the clinic, and it was just by chance, matching walk-in patients without appointments with whatever doctor was free at the moment, that I first met Dr. Joseph Sonnabend. It was 1979, and the "decade gay rights won legitimacy"[1] was about to end. No one knew what was next; all I wanted was more of the same, minus one thing: moments like this. When my name was called, I got up and met the doctor who'd been handed my chart. I had no idea I was meeting my personal Moses, the man who gave me the tools to stay sexually active and safe in the deadliest of days of AIDS and showed me how to dodge disasters that would claim my friends and decimate my generation. All I cared about in those first few moments together was getting whatever pills I needed as fast as I could that would make my cramps instantly disappear and never, ever return. Is that too much to ask?

Dr. Sonnabend explained that there was a growing outbreak of sexually transmitted intestinal parasites that were afflicting the sexually active community, but gay men were being hit hardest. I'd seen articles about it in the gay press, but nothing teaches more effectively than firsthand experience. He said I had to go to a specialized testing laboratory where I had to shit into a cup to determine what type(s) of parasites I had; there were many kinds. If that wasn't detestable enough, my lab results came back positive for three. I was prescribed three expensive medications for thirty days to get rid of them. Then I had to return to the clinic to provide yet another stool sample to make sure the medicines had worked; sometimes they didn't and the whole month of pills had to be repeated and yet another cup provided. This repulsive merry-go-round was not for me. What had happened to a handful of pills, a cup of water, and you're done? Fed up and disgusted, I pleaded with Dr. Sonnabend, "Tell me what I need to do to avoid getting this again, and I swear I'll do it." I felt embarrassed sounding as if I was trying to avoid a fatal disease but was instantly relieved by Dr. Sonnabend's respectful, professorial reply.

He explained that the highest risk for infection with parasites was "rimming," oral/anal contact. I knew for sure that I hadn't contracted parasites that way. Then Dr. Sonnabend explained that giving oral sex to someone after they fucked someone else if they didn't wash well afterward, like in a bar's backroom or a bathhouse, could easily lead to infection.

Bingo! From then on, I was meticulous about what went into my mouth while at the baths. I cruised at the showers to find partners to take back to my room, and before I knew it, showers became foreplay, rooms were for sex. Having parasites was so disgusting I had no choice. I followed one more of Dr. Sonnabend's subsequent recommendations. I started buying germicidal surgical soaps, like Betadine and PhisoHex, to wash up after sex. I was determined to remain sexually active even in the middle of an epidemic of sexually transmitted parasites, and thanks to Dr. Sonnabend, who took the time to educate me, *I never got infected with them again!* The idea that I could modify my sexual behavior to greatly reduce the risk of acquiring STIs was firmly planted in my happy, horny mind.

By the time my escort ads began appearing regularly, four concerns shaped what I would and wouldn't do: an obsession with hygiene; an acute fear of STIs; an ingrained cultural belief that the "passive" or receptive partner in sex was taking the "degrading," "feminine" role; and the fact that there was no way that just any stranger who came along could hand me a sum of money and expect me to fuck him on demand. In New Jersey, "sex" always meant oral sex; it was easy to sit back, fantasize and get serviced for the fifteen or so minutes it usually took Jersey guys to climax. But in Manhattan, "sex" meant fucking; that turned the table, quadrupled the time and meant I had to do the "work." Anal intercourse in a relationship was one thing, but no amount of money could convince my dick to get that job done. Still, I held onto the hope that if I could find my way out of the closet, I could find a way around this.

My concerns quickly faded away. I wasn't sure why but the men who called my ad and decided to hire me after a long conversation all wanted to be "dominated." They seemed flabbergasted on the phone that I had more questions for them than they had for me. Shaken by the murder of my first Manhattan client, I used my sexiest, butchest voice to get the men who called my ad to talk at length about their sexual desires. It was a ruse to weed out cops and danger; any man who was unfamiliar with the gay scene or sounded awkward stating what he liked sexually was firmly told that I wasn't what he was seeking. I knew enough about gay life to detect a gay man when I heard one talking about the best fuck he ever had while I kept pitching questions for more detail in rapid fire. If callers were horny when they dialed my number, they were panting by the time I was satisfied with my erotic interrogation. My forcefulness in flinging questions and my unyielding persistence in making them talk about sex tapped into something inside me that I wasn't fully aware of, but men old enough to be my father were. I exuded a quality that was the essence of a dominant, S&M top.

I attracted men who were more than eager to teach a take-charge twenty-four-year-old with an ample supply of anger how to channel that hostility and release it into S&M. Many bought me leather attire, like chaps, harnesses, studded belts, cock rings, boots, and anything else their fantasies required. Some brought sex toys and accoutrements and left them with me so they didn't have to keep lugging them back. As my apartment started to look like a sex shop, I realized my niche had discovered me. S&M was the perfect antidote to my fear of pain and anti-gay violence, seducing me with the illusion that I could control two dreaded things I couldn't make go away. Ironically, that's how a germaphobic, hygiene-obsessed Jewish boy with performance anxiety and an acute fear of violence took to S&M like a fish to water and came to intimately know many hundreds of men who would soon become the earliest victims of AIDS.

Many of these men told me they had become "tired" with regular, "vanilla" sex. Was that a polite way of saying they'd had enough sex and dick? What comes after that? This was better than grad school. They wanted someone with the masculinity, creativity, and believability to act out scenarios of domination and submission. They didn't want me to obligatorily give them my dick; that was a bore. They wanted me to make them beg for it, to make them "earn" it, and that turned me on so intensely, I had an erection more often than I needed it. What mattered to these men wasn't just the dick, what mattered most to these men was the man behind the dick. They were custom made for my four "concerns" and me. My resentment at being expected to fuck anyone who could pay me met its solution. My dick was a precious commodity; the more I teased and denied the more it sparked a higher demand, the more they begged and panted, the greedier I got. They had to do more than earn it, they had to convince me it was what they lived for and they had to mean it. What clients said they wanted became a starting point; it launched me on journeys I never expected, but the men I took along, kept coming back for more.

Far from my worst fears of becoming a used-up hustler having the life sucked out of him or a "stud" who couldn't get hard, S&M taught me to give myself in measured, precious doses—when the client had "earned" it. Most of the Models/Escorts ads that ran in the *Advocate* classifieds were advertising Tops, but many of those escorts I met in three-ways preferred being bottoms. They lied because the market for gay sex work was the opposite of most heterosexual sex work, where a woman is used and objectified in whatever way a man wanted. With gay prostitution, it was often the clients who wanted to be receptive and, in my case, dominated and sexually used. Many men were telling me about their most seasoned fantasies; I was never at a loss for new ideas. The fantasy that someone explained to me at noon could be bestowed on the client at midnight. I didn't want to get bored any more than they did. At twenty-four, I was a novelty, an erotic prick with a brain. Hardly anyone made it to an hour without climaxing, and once they did, my work was done. If I did my work well, my orgasms could remain mine. I had no trouble getting my sexual needs met elsewhere, and I was so grateful I could have it that way. I wanted to provide a service, not my body and my soul.

Now I knew another reason why I had left Rob. I wanted to live more before I settled down. I wanted to be wild, I wanted to see the world, I wanted to make this arrogant city mine. I wanted to exploit my looks and my youth and my intelligence and see how high I could fly. After eighteen consecutive years of full-time school and part-time jobs, I wanted insanity. I wanted to break every rule. I wanted not to know what I was doing tomorrow or later. I wanted to devour life. And then when I felt enriched with experience, I wanted to settle with someone like Rob or, if possible, Rob himself. He was beginning to see that even though I had left, even though I'd hurt him, I wasn't gone and I never would be. What we had was family and that would never die. He let me know that if we were ever to get back together, I had to be absolutely certain it was for good.

Acting as the "master" meant the gentle, softer side of me was being pushed away yet again—just like when I was in third grade and when I started living in a college dorm. Tenderness is seen as weakness in a man and vulnerability not a value, but it sure fills the coffers. With the help of wonderfully supportive hustlers I met in three-ways, I drafted a new ad marketing myself as an "experienced 24-year-old Italian S&M Topman"; a client suggested I add, "who gets off on using you." Smart man—those were the six words that made business boom.

In the spirit of Uta Hagen's *Respect for Acting,* I developed a character, a persona, and an attitude: macho, arrogant, and sexually self-absorbed. The qualities I'd come to loathe in men were now my playful, erotic arsenal. When friends were at my apartment and I got a phone call from the new ad, they freaked out watching my Jekyll and Hyde transformation into a tough-as-nails Top as soon as I picked up the phone. They called him Vinnie.

With my jet-black hair, dark eyes, and a suntan I began replenishing every few months in Miami, almost everyone I met assumed I was Italian and praised me for it so I went along with how clients wanted to see me. So many escort ads in the *Advocate* said "hot Italian," but you never saw anyone advertising as a "hot Jew." I didn't think of Vinnie as lying or hiding my Judaism: Vinnie was commerce. I put him on like a business suit to go to work. I regarded Vinnie as erotic license, as in artistic license; running a titillating S&M scene felt like my newfound erotic art. It was constantly changing and evolving and as soon as I summed it up and explained it to friends one way, I ended moving into unexpected areas another way.

I understood why it was difficult for men to reveal the human desire to relinquish control in sex because it transgressed our culture's definition of what it meant to be a man in much the same way that homosexuality did: that transgression was its main source of erotic power. The more forbidden the desire, the more pleasure there was to be found. With my new boldly stated ad, what many men had been searching for night after night cruising in bars could be discreetly purchased and obtained as easily as going to a convenience store for sex. I knew most people would regard me as a whore, a pervert, a sleazy fag, but I'd become inured to all of that from being gay. My years in a loving, monogamous relationship didn't alter the infuriating, ubiquitous perception that gay sex of any kind was "an abomination," a "crime against nature." As I wrapped my earnings with elastic bands into $1,000 stacks, I realized that learning to live with that taught me to live with this. The radical politics of being a gay activist in the 1970s paved the way to radical sex in the 1980s, but I didn't know the meaning of radical till I woke up to the nightmare waiting for me at the end of this road.

Gay liberation had raised my consciousness, but it became my springboard into absolute craziness. It woke me up to a world where people are crippled in their ability see my humanity because of my sexuality, leaving me with two choices. First, to fight for change, which I did through college. But as I watched on TV as Ronald Reagan moved closer to inhabiting the White House, I was utterly convinced that our well-intentioned battles for gay rights were now helping to ensure Reagan's election. Gays wanted so badly to be accepted and embraced, but the country was not ready. We terrified people who were taught to hate homosexuality and fear change. I understood: I used to be one of them. But now, I didn't care at all about normalcy. The millionaires I was meeting couldn't care less what anyone thought about their sexual habits, it was only the middle class that was constantly worrying about sexual respectability. Gays were ipso facto not respectable, so why not see that as invitation to sexual freedom? Now that I had money, I saw another option. Accept what you can't alter and drown life's intractable disappointments in as much pleasure and fun as America offers to those who can afford it. I was ready to do that with a vengeance. I had more cash than I knew what to do with and the greatest city on earth was right outside my door. This was the time of my life to have fun; if anyone didn't want to hear bad news about the gay lifestyle, it was me, taking it to new extremes.

A client who had inherited a chain of dairies and bought me a stereo system kept mailing me pages from *GQ* with money and a note saying, "You'd look hot in this." It was a clarion call to shopping. Manhattan was a movie lover's heaven and a paradise for fine dining. I could treat my friends to Broadway shows and plane tickets to come join me in Miami Beach. Rob and I loved smoking pot and doing tourist things like taking the Circle Line around Manhattan, going to the top of the Empire State Building and the World Trade Center, and seeing every new exhibit at museums. I loved not knowing what part of the city I'd end up in each time I had an outcall. It was fun to see the inside of the best hotels and luxurious suites, to have sex on penthouse rooftops with breathtaking views, and wander home in awe of every block teeming with activity and life in this magnificent city that never seemed to sleep. The time to be rich is when you're young, full of wonder and energy, and feeling gorgeous. I had worked at McDonald's, the loading docks in Port Elizabeth, and more minimum wage jobs than I care to remember. I knew a good gig when I found it, and I savored the rich and radical life of being a worshipped Rent-a-Master. America made me feel like an outcast, so outcast this!

Some clients just wanted to get played with; I'd been taught how to do it well and kept discovering my own ways of doing it better. I took great pleasure from making men moan in ecstasy and quickly rounded up appropriate, unobtrusive background music to drown out their wails from my neighbors. Luckily, I lived in the back of a tenement building inhabited by elderly ladies and older gay men who got along well and didn't mind my traffic. "Your visitors are so polite," a knowing seventy-year-old woman told me: "They carry my grocery bags up to my floor." Only in New York City, I thought. "It's amazing your door is still on its hinges," said the gay painter across the hall.

Although I had experienced ecstatic anal pleasure having mutual intercourse with Rob, I never thought deeply about it, but I realized now that Nature must have intended for men to be fucked or there wouldn't be the tremendous capacity for anal orgasms. While younger, more radical members of the women's movement were reclaiming and celebrating clitoral orgasms and realizing that penis-fucking wasn't the only or even the best way to achieve them, it was as if many gay men were busy discovering that the other half of their penis was inside their rectum. When Jane Fonda mounted Jon Voight for sex in the movie *Coming Home*, you knew traditional, heterosexual, missionary position, woman-on-bottom, man-on-top intercourse was being turned on its head. This was the real sexual revolution: Clitoral and anal orgasms were shaking everything up.[2]

The difference between men and women didn't seem like the polar opposites that I was raised to believe in, even though women always bore the burden of consequences from sex to a degree that men never seemed to fully or even remotely comprehend. I couldn't help but wonder if patriarchy kept men ignorant of the pleasures to be found in receptive anal sex; it certainly narrowed the gap between gender in my eyes. And so, what started as a quest for quick cash became a mission. Sex was an important human need and being a student of life in the fast lane during the peak of the sexual revolution fascinated me. Seeing so many men pursuing a culturally forbidden sexual desire to be receptive, open, submissive, and passive was a window on part of the male experience I loved seeing. We swim in a sea of lies every day, from advertising to politicians to salesmen, but when men pay for sex, you get the truth about what some men want, and the truth, especially when it comes to sex, is harder to find than you think.

In my circle of friends from New Jersey, I'd been the radical activist; I was now the radical slut. Most of them were in relationships, some open, some having three-ways, some fighting to stay monogamous amid so much temptation. I was the only one who could afford an apartment in the city so it became a twenty-four-hour community center. Friends would plan what clubs to go to as they fixed their hair, danced to the latest disco hits, helped themselves to whatever drugs clients left behind, and crashed after all-night bar hopping. I loved putting my friends in bondage and taking Polaroids of them buried in a pile of sex toys. I often hid them in one room while seeing a client in another.

The ethos of the late '70s was "Try it, you'll like it," but if you were frightened, or didn't want to even try something new, then something was wrong with you. If there was an aspect of sexuality that you didn't understand and people kept telling you how it gave them pleasure, who were you to judge? That's how straight people oppressed gays. So, since I felt obligated as a Top who was being paid, I learned as clients taught me how to give pleasure in the erotic art of anal stimulation, also known as ass play. I was giving pleasure in ways I never dreamed possible thanks, in large part, to a sweeping gay male trend.

Douching—taking an enema to wash away any trace of feces before engaging in receptive anal sex—had become routine for most sexually active gay men. "Feminine hygiene products" began being advertised on television in the '70s. At first they caused an uproar; some felt that they were "distasteful." But missing from that debate was that it gave a lot of gay men the idea to hose and clean their own "pussy." As a Top for hire, I was endlessly grateful for that.

At the same time, I began noticing that more and more of my friends were getting infected with herpes. Seeing puss oozing out of sores on their lips led me to subtly examine my sexual partners and clients, but there was no way to eliminate the risk, only to be on the lookout for it. My gratitude for discovering S&M deepened as it required the least amount of actual sex. I was glad I didn't have to make love or reciprocate oral and anal sex with anyone who had the cash. Not that I didn't, but it had to be when I desired it, too. Hustling intelligently led me to take the easy way out and that reduced my risk for herpes and other STIs.

It seemed like once some men discovered the pleasures of anal sex that was all they wanted to do. Many business executives told me, "All day long at work I'm telling everyone what to do; I'm in control. When I come to you, make me do what you want." I felt there was some truth to that, but truth in sex is always more complicated. I knew I had to "want" to dominate them or they wouldn't come back. All that talk about the pressures of being in control at work sounded like an excuse for not being able to come right out and say, I want to be fucked but without feeling less of a man. Clients had to believe I needed and wanted to do what I did and not because I was being paid. As I watched some Wall Street executive crawl around my floor moaning like a dog in heat, I couldn't help but think, "All day long you're screwing people over for money, jockeying for power and ordering your secretary around. Then you come here and turn it into a game you can stop whenever you want." I didn't feel good about that, so I whacked them on the butt to relieve my frustration, but that only turned them on more.

What was this manipulative and desperate search for a Master or Daddy that I was fulfilling for men twice my age? Maybe because my father had been affectionate and loving, I didn't feel that driving need. I never told people this because I didn't want genuine, healthy, and all too rare affection between men misinterpreted as repressed homosexuality, but my father woke me up in the morning by kissing my forehead. On a visit home to my mother, looking through family photo albums, I was struck by how comfortable my father appeared in picture after picture hugging me, holding me, carrying me, and kissing me. Even as a child, when I looked around at other people's fathers, I was grateful for mine. What I heard from some of my clients elevated that appreciation even higher.

Many told me stories of feeling emotionally starved and crippled by having fathers who they felt didn't know how to express love or show them affection. Maybe that kind of male "tough love" was just an excuse for men who found it tough *to love*. At the end of many of my scenes, after the client would climax, I wanted to bend down and scoop him up in my arms and just hold him. In time, I did. I guess it was kind of like therapy for some of them, as more than a few would actually begin to whimper. Maybe in some way I was helping them to exorcise some kind of cultural or familial demons. Several times I was told that coming to see me replaced going to see their therapist.

Or was I kidding myself? Nothing blinds like money. Why did so many men's sexuality focus on being used and on verbal and physical degradation? Was I reinforcing gay self-hatred, or in some way diminishing it by channeling it into a sexual outlet, a source of pleasure and gratification. I didn't have the answer, but everything I did was consenting and could be stopped at any time simply by asking me.

It seemed like everyone was busy exploring and having more sex; women had greater birth control options for protection and gay men had antibiotics for syphilis and gonorrhea. Growing up in a misogynist culture had to encourage homosexual desire even as our schizophrenic culture punished homosexual sex. Galvanized by a sexy and cocky new visibility that emerged in the late '70s, many urban gay men were discarding impotent politics to act on any and every sexual desire that came our way. Our slogans "An army of lovers cannot lose" and "a brotherhood of lust" were replaced by "So many men, so little time." Every taboo had to be challenged, every limit pushed. We weren't going to get our civil rights anytime soon, but on the dance floor or in the ever more crowded backrooms, it was easy to dream that somehow we could dance and fuck our way to liberation. Pop a quaalude and see.

I began to see something enlightening, liberating, and yet disturbing in the S&M scenes I was doing: Sexuality was not some fixed, unchanging biologically determined force of nature as I had come to see it in my gay/straight, either/or view of the world. It was to some degree socially constructed by the culture we grew up in. Our society was fucked up about sex, and we were products of that society, so why shouldn't some of our sexual expression reflect that? Maybe Gore Vidal had it partly right when he saw S&M as a product of "the powerlessness that most people feel in an overpopulated and overorganized society . . . a symptom of helplessness."[3]

Were by-products of America's racism, sexism, homophobia, and greed being played out through sexual tension on the floor of my apartment?

"Take it bitch! Yeah, you want that fuckin' dick, faggot. Lick my boots, you worthless slave. You want more—don't you, pig!" This is what my clients had taught me to say, and the power I felt guiding these forbidden carnal journeys was electrifying. There was often something cathartic about reclaiming those words and epithets while sexually acting out cultural conflicts and tensions. After many clients climaxed, the play was over, the curtain came down, and I held them in my arms while they drifted back to reality from afterglow. Then came the difficult moment of decision: Do I offer affection or will it be a turnoff? It was so bizarre: Fornication was a breeze while simple human affection remained so awkward until a client broke the ice or gave a sign he wanted it. But as time went on and my pool of regulars grew, so did the hugs and kisses.

But not every man who hired me wanted a hug good-bye. There were also those who departed with the same insecure, dispirited postures they entered with, for whom S&M seemed rooted in their conviction that they deserved contempt instead of love. For them, life was a walk of shame; they departed the way they entered. The adage, "We'd rather be praised than punished, but we'd rather be punished than ignored," summed up the sad side of the market for my new career.

The sexual revolution that began in the '60s taught us that sex and love didn't always have to be the same thing. Sex could be an ultimate expression of love, a form of play and communication, a human need to merge with another, an art. It could also be very serious business. It was often hot that way—focused, intense, and ecstatic. After many of my S&M scenes were over, I noticed that happy bounce in my clients' step mentioned in the best book written about this era, Edmund White's *States of Desire*. In it, White theorized that maybe

S&M sex "so thoroughly drain[s] off the normal human reservoir of nastiness that [participants] emerge as relatively benign beings." I wanted to believe that exploring S&M, which I enjoyed, which paid well, and which gave me enormous social mobility, could also provide insights into what our particular culture was doing to some of our hearts and minds. I was a product and an outcast of American society—was that what made S&M and sex work feel like home? I was in business, providing quick, reliable, consumerist sex for a consumerist culture. Welcome to McVinnie's. I'll take your fucking order.

Hustling was an exciting, pleasure-filled adventure.

I felt like a great explorer, hacking my way through uncharted sexual territory, not knowing exactly what I would find, but compelled to continue the search. I wasn't looking to conquer foreign lands, subordinate natives, or plunder natural resources—I just wanted to try and understand some of the mysteries of sex and to make money. There were so many lies, myths, and secrets surrounding sex that caused so much anxiety and human misery. In *Pleasure and Danger: Exploring Female Sexuality*, Dorothy Allison's essay, "Public Silence, Private Terror," raised my awareness even more with a cry from the female sphere: "When we speak about sex, grief should not be where we have to start."[4] Why does it have to be this way?

And yet, what was a sensitive guy like me doing stomping around night and day in black leather and boots? Was it my defensive overreaction to the stereotype of gay men as weak and sissyish? What happened to that softer man feminism and the early gay libbers wanted to free? Is that him on his knees, handcuffed, and aching to be used? Gay liberation was supposed to be about men loving men, I thought, as I watched a client diligently licking my boots. Maybe what I was selling was the message of the Moral Majority turned into sex play. Was the volume of my business rising in correlation to the religious right? What exactly was this "pleasure" that I was selling?

S&M wouldn't stand still. It was a constant, internal tug of war. It felt positive exploring and playing with power, and sometimes there was a fine line between pleasure and pain, but when someone just wanted to be degraded or abused, I finally learned to just say no; it was too depressing. I was making mistakes along the way, but I felt that sex was the way gay men felt more fully alive in a world where so many wanted us eradicated. It was a clever, little insight until I realized it applied to me.

During the day, bored-to-death friends would call me from work, complaining about being trapped behind some desk, waiting for the clock to turn five. "You're so lucky," they'd drool, "I have to smile and kiss ass all day long to keep my shitty job and you're worried that *you* feel like a whore?" It made me feel so free. When a client asked me what time I got up in the morning, I said, "When I feel like it." Half the time I didn't even know what day it was. Calendars and clocks had become irrelevant to me. Every day, every hour was a good time for sex play and pay.

Life seemed so sweet. My regular clients were like a parade of human diversity traipsing through my apartment night and day, bearing gifts, champagne, cash, and a hunger for pleasure and fun. I was treated to a shopping spree on Rodeo Drive and a trip to Paris and was flown around the country. But I always bailed out early to get back to my friends as soon as my "work" moved from play to filling a loneliness many men had.

For me, gay life in New York City before the dawn of AIDS was like living in the Promised Land. I went dancing almost every night. There were always exciting places in Manhattan to see and be seen, night-and-day sex at the piers off West Street, backroom bars and sex clubs that were packed till dawn. Whatever fantasy you had, you always knew you could satisfy it any time, night or day, at one of the many sexual playgrounds. And always, everywhere gay men congregated, there was that infectious, pulsing disco beat, pouring out of the bars and clubs and into the streets where beautiful men, new kids in town, and free sidewalk drag shows colored the center of gay life on Christopher Street. Although it often seemed like sex was becoming the only glue that held gay men together, sex often led to enduring friendships and even relationships; but it was hard staying focused on one person for long when you were living in a bustling sexual amusement park. The commercialization of urban gay male life was taking over as new bars, discos, and sex clubs competed for gay dollars by offering more enticing and more expensive places to drink and connect for quick, anonymous sex in between beers and chatting with friends. In the midst of that fervor, I'd set up shop as an escort at the perfect age and time. When Hollywood made a movie about the urban disco scene called *Saturday Night Fever, Christopher Street* magazine shot back with a cover story titled "Every Night Fever." That captured life for many of us inside the urban gay ghetto.

Being a young successful hustler in Manhattan felt like a dream come true. The real American gigolo was gay. My only concern was where were we going and where did it end?

          ⋘   ⋙

The urban gay disco scene reached new heights of hedonism and breathtaking beauty when a planetarium-like disco called the Saint opened in September 1980 in New York City. A close friend named Mike, an artist and fellow escort, designed the poster for the grand opening night party, a hallmark event few there would forget.

Nothing compared to the experience of dancing till dawn with Rob and my friends while disco divas like Grace Jones performed live under the Saint's colossal, hi-tech, semispherical ceiling of the night sky filled with twinkling stars, shooting stars, flying comets, and laser lights. Surrounded by the hottest men imaginable all dancing to the most meticulously chosen music that wouldn't let you stand still for hours, everyone seemed high and happy under the pleasure dome. Urban gay male life had evolved over a decade from personal salvation into a communal identity and now, as the Saint became our weekly Mecca, into a quasi-religion. Several thousand muscled, shirtless gay men in black 501 jeans all danced a Native American–like disco war dance in unison every weekend, almost all weekend long. Upstairs was a huge darkened balcony converted into carpeted bleachers where hundreds of stoned men fucked all night and into the next day. To lose oneself so completely, in the wall-to-wall men moaning in the dark or pounding the dance floor, swept away by the tribal beat of the music, basking in the loveliest, acid-enhanced lights, soaring on a hit of ethyl chloride while friends grabbed you with tears of joy in their eyes and comets flew overhead, was like being transported to some heavenly other planet somewhere beyond the stars.

By 1981, there was a growing informal network of local gay drug dealers who would hand you a long menu, as detailed as a restaurant, of available party and sex drugs when you went to make your purchases before the weekend. Since every day of my life was the weekend, I could always beat the Friday rush when dealers ran dry. An idolized porn star, who lived a block from me, made deliveries. He dressed up like a working-class handyman on his rounds and carried an army green metal toolbox that was neatly filled with different drugs in all the little compartments. One dealer on Bank Street greeted customers naked in his bed sitting next to a can of lubricant and stoned out of his mind. If you were willing to play with him for a while, you didn't have to pay. But the air in his apartment was choking with the stench of rancid Crisco, and he was such an unfocused mess, I wanted to throw in a tip if he'd toss my order across the room. I didn't know why I was drawn to returning to him. I guess it made me feel superior seeing someone like that and knowing (or was it hoping?) that it would never happen to me. Stories began circulating about popular guys overdosing in the baths and backrooms.

One Sunday morning, after a busy night of clients, I pushed myself to see one more at 6 A.M. He was an easygoing guy, so I did a line a coke and yanked my boots back on. They were looking worn. I'd worked hard that night so when he pressed me to join him in doing some Ecstasy, I relented. The high was so incredible I felt consumed by a voracious and uninhibited sexual hunger and it had nothing to do with being a top. I couldn't wait for him to leave so I could take that high to the baths. You don't get parasites from getting fucked. I was deluding myself about herpes but this was too extraordinary to care.

But what goes up, eventually comes down, in the form of a chemical crash. I was working hard and making so much money, but where was it getting me? The time to return for my master's degree had come and gone without my even noticing. At the same time, I felt more alienated than ever by the growing affection many Americans had for President Reagan. In response to a reporter about his administration's decision to cut school lunch programs and the effect that might have on the health of the poor, Reagan actually said, as is widely known, "Ketchup is a vegetable." His demonization of the poor and his policies to make America strong by essentially throwing the weak overboard didn't seem to hinder many Americans from feeling a renewed patriotism.

In my circle of friends, I could see our cynicism growing deeper. When New York City's gay rights ordinance went down in defeat for the tenth year in a row, *Village Voice* columnist Arthur Bell wrote in the November 25, 1982, issue, "A common attitude of the gay on the street is, 'Fuck them all. I'll live my life without it.' The gay-on-the-run has given up on politics, organizations, zaps and formal gay liberation. Liberation in the early '80s is internal. Check Saturday night at the Saint."

Bell was a hero to me, the first out-of-the-closet mainstream American reporter who entertained or kicked ass on a weekly basis, but I wondered if, at forty-eight, he fully understood the youthful scene at the Saint that was replacing gay men's involvement in political organizing. He must have seen gay magazines publish accounts such as this one. "The darkness, the dankness, the sleaziness merely added to the excitement. It's crowded and you can feel a stranger standing beside you, his body pressed hard against yours. You move into him, and as your buns respond to the urgency of his swelling cock, you undo your belt and zipper and drop your pants to the floor. Then he's inside you, fucking you, and someone is on his knees giving you some of the best head you've ever had. . . . You're trembling all over. Your knees are nearly giving way. It's hot. You're sweaty. Someone shoves a popper up your nose. You see fucking sunrise. Where are you? You shoot your wad down the guy's neck, and the stranger explodes his load inside your ass. . . . [I]t was good. And the audience *loved* it."[5]

⇐   ⇒

My fear of herpes got company. As more and more of my friends suffered through bouts with hepatitis, I knew my time was drawing closer. I'd never been really sick or hospitalized and I dreaded getting ill.

On July 31, 1981, I woke up feeling like death. I went to pee and saw my urine come out brownish. I looked in the mirror and saw that I was jaundiced. Here it was at last, hepatitis, and I hated it. I dragged myself to Dr. Sonnabend's office on West 12th Street, where he took some blood and told me to go home and stay in bed until it passed. I had never felt so miserably sick in all my life and what depressed me even more was realizing I could get hepatitis again; there were now A, B, and a new strain called C.

"You *must* call all your sexual partners and tell them to get a gammaglobulin shot to prevent them from getting sick," Sonnabend ordered. Most guys laughed or rolled their eyes whenever he said that—How do you contact a body from a darkened balcony? But not for me: I kept a record and Sonnabend's earnest plea, which seemed to belong to a more innocent time gone by, fell on receptive ears this time. I wouldn't evade my responsibility.

I went through my log of all the clients I had seen that month and began calling them. I felt awful, but amazingly, everyone thanked me for calling. If they were angry, they didn't show it; I would have been, but no one I knew was as neurotic as me about STIs. It was a good thing that I kept precise records, although the main reason was that there was such a flurry of men, sometimes I couldn't remember who I had seen a few days before, let alone last month. I knew business kept growing, but as I went down the list of men I might have exposed to hepatitis, I began to feel uneasy. Where did I get the energy? Oh yeah, cocaine. It was a lot of men, a lot of sex, and more and more drugs, and it hurt to see I was running myself ragged. I saved the hardest call for last. It was to a client named Joe, who had come to me every day that month and we were planning a trip to Cuernavaca.

"It's not your fault," he said after belting out a groan, "it's just that I've already had hepatitis twice and my doctor told me my liver can't take much more. I drink a lot and the coke is bad, too. I know what to do. Pack a bag of clothes and I'll take you to my country house in New Hope. You need to eat well to get better. I'll make you gourmet meals and you can just stay in bed until this passes." I made a mental note to never forget that S&M and love can coexist as I packed my bag.

In an hour he picked me up—and brought along a videocassette recorder, which had just come out on the market, and shopping bag filled with my favorite movies. He cooked for me, convinced me to smoke pot, which replaced my nausea with hunger, and five days later I was feeling better. Still, just the thought of sex and drugs made me want to puke.

A week later I was back home feeling shaken but healed. I went to see a new gay German movie called *Taxi Zum Klo,* which was chosen to premiere as part of the prestigious New York film festival. The opening credits translated the title into "Taxi to the Toilet." This, I thought excitedly, was going to be a wonderfully radical gay movie.

Halfway into the film, I discovered that the title came from a scene where the gay protagonist is hospitalized for hepatitis, but still feels horny, so he tucks his hospital gown into his jeans and sneaks out. He takes a cab to the local public toilets where he has sex with a stranger—while he's still sick and contagious. The sex scene involves a very funny physical comedy bit about his full-length hospital gown, which was tucked deep into his pants. The guy going to suck him tries pulling his shirt out of his jeans, but the "shirt" appears endless as he keeps pulling it out and out and out of his pants, seemingly with no end. The predominantly gay audience roared in laughter, but with my own jaundice freshly faded, I felt like the only one in that theater who was definitely not laughing. Something felt gravely wrong both on the screen and in the audience.

I started asking myself some hard questions when I left the theater. Was getting more hepatitis and someday herpes just inevitable, something to resign myself to? No amount of money was worth that, but what was I going to do? This was fall 1981 in New York City—the gay capital of the world. If I had learned anything in my life, it was that this was the time and the place to party. Surely I'd stop hustling in a couple of years or certainly before I turned thirty.

A month later, Dr. Sonnabend called me to come to his office. He said we needed to talk. During my appointment, I noticed that my medical folder was becoming disturbingly thick as Dr. Sonnabend began showing me my test results.

"Well you definitely had hepatitis A, your liver functions were sky high, and you've also been exposed to hepatitis B and probably fought it off without realizing you had it. Luckily, you're not a carrier. Syphilis was negative but you've also been exposed recently to CMV, cytomegalovirus, and that could reactivate Epstein-Barr virus, which causes mono. Have you felt tired lately?"

What a disconcerting mouthful poured out of him. "Tired? I run around a lot but I don't feel sick. I do have this bump under my ear but it doesn't hurt and it's probably nothing." He reached over to feel it with a look of unnerving intensity.

"That's a swollen gland. Lift up your arms so I can check for more. Here's another one and another one and another one."

He was making me nervous and nauseous and scared.

"Look, your blood counts aren't normal and you've got swollen glands."

"But I'm getting over hepatitis. Give my body some time to heal. I'll come back in a month and do the blood tests again."

I didn't return for three months, until December, and when the new results came back, he told me I was immune deficient—whatever that meant—and then he said the unthinkable: "Stop fucking around!"

Stop fucking around? Just stop? How could I? My whole life revolved around sex. I looked at Sonnabend with the sincerest look I could muster and nodded my head in feigned acquiescence.

"I want to arrange for a lymph node biopsy."

"Have a gland cut out of my neck?" I asked in horror.

"It's not that bad and it's the only way to know if you have something."

"Have something like what?" I mumbled in mortification. But before he could answer I said, "Listen, I have to think about this."

I couldn't wait to get out of there. Biopsies are for cancer. How could a doctor specializing in sexually transmitted diseases tell me to stop having sex? He needs to get out of that office more often.

But I had to keep going back. I was really getting into being fucked at the baths on Ecstasy; the drug just obliterated all my inhibitions. But I got gonorrhea after every single trip, and I had to go back to Sonnabend for antibiotics. All I had to do was swallow some pills to get rid of it, so what's the big deal?

There was a network of what gay men affectionately called "clap doctors" in New York City whose practices arose in response to the homophobic attitudes of straight physicians as well as the ever-rising incidences of sexually transmitted diseases in most large cities. Among fast-lane gay men, it had become a compliment to be called a hot "sex pig," and most of us had our own clap doctors we believed in and took our sexual partners to. I loved that Sonnabend's attitude was completely professional even though he was quite unorthodox. His background was more as a research scientist than just a physician. I adored the fact that he, on several occasions, gave office jobs he had available to guys who seemed in most need of work: radical fairies, semi-neurotics, gay men who were so beaten down by life they had no trace of self-esteem, fluttering around the office like butterflies or crying because someone said something that "wasn't very nice." There was something compassionate and endearing about Sonnabend. He spent time really listening to me; he asked more questions than I did. After my first appointment at his office, he inquired if I had health insurance and when I said no, he replied, "Then pay what you can," and disappeared. That, I thought, is a true doctor. My father and he would have gotten along famously. I couldn't leave him.

"You can't keep coming in here every month with gonorrhea in your butt. You've got to stop what you're doing!"

"Why don't you give me some antibiotics to take before I go to the baths so I won't get gonorrhea; so many guys are doing that."

"That won't protect you from viruses. I'll give you some," he said angrily, "but only if you promise me to go get that gland out."

"I will . . . soon," I said, and hurried home with my new prescription, happy that the next time I went to the baths, I wouldn't have to face him three days after.

There was a rumor making its way around the hustler grapevine about Hibiscus, a gender-bending performance artist I knew; we shared a rich client who paid for him to advertise his music group on the billboard over Village Cigars in Sheridan Square. He was sick with a new mysterious disease; it was no big deal—it was just a handful of gay guys getting it, but St. Vincent's Hospital sent him home dying because he had no health insurance. I had read about the new gay disease in a new local gay newspaper called the *New York Native*. It was just a small number of cases and no reason to freak out.

But on May 11, 1982, the *New York Times* reported, "New Homosexual Disorder Worries Health Officials," with a more ominous take.

> A serious disorder of the immune system that has been known to doctors for less than a year—a disorder that appears to affect primarily male homosexuals—has now afflicted at least 335 people, of whom it has killed 136. . . . Federal health officials are concerned that tens of thousands more homosexual men may be silently affected and therefore vulnerable to potentially grave ailments. . . . Researchers call it AID, for acquired immune deficiency disease, or GRID, for gay-related immunodeficiency. It has been reported in 20 states and seven countries. But the overwhelming majority of cases have been in New York City. . . .

Reading that haunted me; I was sorry I did. A few weeks later, I met the hottest man at the Rawhide bar in my neighborhood. Just as I was about to take him home, he suddenly looked suspicious and said, "What is that bump under your ear?"

I was stunned. I could feel the earth quaking all around me as Sonnabend's pleas and warnings began echoing in my mind. The man bid me good night and left me leaning on the Pac Man machine feeling like an abandoned leper. When I gathered myself, I noticed a brochure display on the bar with pamphlets about the Gay Men's Health Crisis. I stuck one in my back pocket and left the bar.

While walking solemnly home, I was struck with a brilliant idea: Have the swollen gland taken out like Sonnabend wanted, and then when the scar heals I can go back to the Rawhide, find that man and put all this behind me.

Sonnabend referred me to a lymphadenopathy specialist to evaluate me before doing the biopsy. While he was examining my armpits and groin for swollen glands, I figured I'd save him some time. "I don't care about those swollen glands." Pointing to the one protruding under my ear, I said, "This is the only one I want taken out."

"That's the last one I would remove. It's near too many nerves and there would be a risk of facial paralysis."

Facial paralysis? When I got home I jumped under the covers in my bed wondering how to get out of the biopsy. I'll call and say, "Dr. Davis, cancel my biopsy. I don't care about cancer—I only came to see you to get rid of the bump under my ear because it's really bad for cruising." I laughed and then I went numb.

My hairdresser friend Joe called to tell me that his lover's friend Nicky was sick and staying with them.

"What's he got?" I asked.

"What's he *got*?" Joe exclaimed. "What doesn't he got? I wouldn't know where to begin! He's got these purple spots all over his body and face that don't look good."

"Is it that new disease?" I asked ever so delicately.

"He thinks he caught something in the Jacuzzi in Key West, but after doin' acid at the baths for fifteen years, how can he tell? I told you guys those places were no good, but you all laughed. Nicky always said he didn't want to be an old queen and . . . he won't."

At newsstands, it was hard to avoid the *Native* cover stories about a new "gay cancer." A new killer virus was going around and quickly killing some gay men. But it was only a handful of deaths in a city of thousands, so even though it sounded scary, it was no big deal . . . unless, maybe, if you're a hustler having sex with hundreds of gay men. Were those purple spots I kept seeing on clients like Nicky's?

For the biopsy, I was given a painful shot to the back of my neck to numb the area where there was a swollen gland the lymphadenopathy specialist decided to remove. Although I couldn't feel any more pain, I could vividly feel the surgical scissors cutting through my skin like a piece of wet cloth, and I began to weep uncontrollably. When the procedure ended, I went into a staircase and broke down crying.

When I got home, my neighbor had left the new *Advocate* at my door. I checked to see where my escort ad was running. It was listed near the ad for Hibiscus. He was dead, but his ad was still running—right next to mine.

Almost no one knew he had been the antiwar hippie in the famous *Life* magazine photo from the '60s, placing daisies in the gun barrels of the National Guard.

I knew and I knew what I had to do. I called New York Telephone and told them to disconnect both of my numbers. The party that had become my life was over.

3

Stop the World

i may be dying

Dressed for work, July 1982

In my haste to disconnect my phones and detach myself from a lifestyle that was clearly killing me, I was left without phone service for three days until a new number could be activated. The dizzying, hectic pace of my life as a hustler came screeching to a dead halt after two and a half years. The three small rooms of my apartment, which only days before stood as my shrine to the gay male hedonism of the '70s, now began to feel like a cursed Egyptian tomb with the walls closing in on me. My many mirrors, strategically placed for sex, were now reflecting the stark white bandage on my neck, an inescapable sign of my impending doom. This wasn't even an operation—just a biopsy—but I felt like I'd been mutilated. I was anxious to see what it looked like under the bandage, but I feared passing out if I peeked. I wandered dazed around the apartment from room to room, collapsing in tears on my platform bed. How many more gruesome medical procedures lay ahead? Even trying to sleep felt like a morbid rehearsal for the grave. Over and over, I kept playing an old Nina Simone album called *Baltimore;* the somber music and the pain conveyed in her voice made me feel less alone: Someone else had known this despair and found a way to transform it into art. But this was too unbearable: to wither away and die in my twenties. The sounds of the city came crashing through my windows like hurled obscenities, taunting me with the fact that life in Manhattan was hurrying along on its merry way, as if nothing had happened, as if nothing had changed. But it had: I was dying, and gay life as I knew and loved it was over. I wanted the whole city and everyone in it to just come to a stop.

I always knew that when the time came for me to confront a serious illness, the sissy inside me that I stomped down into the deepest recesses of my soul would come bolting out. Like many people, I grew up in a family that never knew how to accept death. Stories I heard about what people had to endure on chemotherapy led me to soothe my fears by joking that when my time came I could swallow some pills and neatly commit suicide before ever going through something as brutal as that. I was so vain about my looks and my hair, I often joked, "I'd rather rot away from cancer than lose my 'coif' to chemo," but I was only half-kidding. I'd come to see myself as a tough, proud fag, a butch, cocky hustler; but somewhere along the way, the real me had gotten lost in the act. The fear of dying wiped all that away, reducing me to a helpless scared little boy, a crybaby.

My death was going to devastate my family and reconfirm their hatred of homosexuality, which only my two brothers knew about. I felt such regret about the choices I had made in my life—not about being gay—that was a Holy, Divine given, but rather, about my promiscuous lifestyle. Was this what I had left Rob and walked away from a real chance at lasting love for? Was this what I marched and protested for? I took down the steel chains, which hung in the archway between my two main rooms, and I threw them into the closet in my backroom. So this is how the journey ends.

After three days alone in bed with only Nina Simone to soothe me, I had scratched the record so badly the stereo needle was skipping through all the songs. In spite of its being August, I put on a turtleneck to hide my bandage, and headed to Crazy Eddie's on 8th Street to buy a new copy. When I got there, I saw a young gay guy strolling down an aisle with a fresh white bandage on the side of his neck exactly like mine. It was startling to see I wasn't alone. I wanted to call out to him, to go over, and tell him, "Me too!" But I froze as I watched him leave. How did it become so easy to fuck each other while remaining so difficult just to say hello?

Heading home through the streets of the West Village, I kept passing gay men and wondering how long it would take for them to realize what was happening. Only days before, my own denial had allowed me to delude myself into thinking that twenty-six-year-olds don't die this way, yet here I was, my hands fluttering self-consciously around my turtleneck, concealing my first battle scar in the soon-to-be full-fledged war of AIDS. The gay ghetto I had come to call home felt like it was turning chaotically upside down like the ship in *The Poseidon Adventure*. Here I was dying, and these innocent fools are still cruising me. I felt more alone hurrying through the crowd on Sixth Avenue than I did during three days isolated in my apartment. There was only one person I knew who would understand. I had to go see Dr. Sonnabend.

His waiting room was so jammed, gay men overflowed into the hallway and lobby of the co-op apartment building where Sonnabend had his practice. My friend Rich once said, "Pills, shots and appointments aren't pleasant but don't lose sight of all the fun we have. Once in a while you gotta pay the piper." But as trips to Sonnabend's office kept increasing in frequency and the risks of more STIs kept increasing, how did I end up going along when I had started out so cautious? Hepatitis didn't stop me. Would herpes have? Those were the two wake-up calls that it wasn't true anymore, that women had the pill, gay men had antibiotics, and modern medicine could cure anything we got. What a grand delusion it had turned out to be. It was hopeless—that's why I didn't want to wake up. Science could never find a cure for this new disease in time to save me.

When Sonnabend came out of the examination room and saw me, he came right over. "Your phone was disconnected. I was worried. I've been trying to get a hold of you to see how the biopsy went. I asked people to go and ring your doorbell to see if you were okay. I would have come myself, but look what's going on here."

I was moved and should have thanked him, but all I could do was yank him close to me and whisper the all-consuming question: "Am I dying?"

Sonnabend took a deep breath and theatrically collapsed on his exhale. As he looked into my eyes, he realized I'd finally seen the light: I'd woken up to the nightmare. After months of trying to get me to change my sexual behavior, he could see in my terrified face that the biopsy had finally shattered my wall of denial.

"Come on, quickly, let's get some coffee," he said.

We walked to the luncheonette at the corner of 12th Street and Sixth Avenue without saying a word, but I couldn't stand the silence: Death is silence. "Am I going to die?" I blurted it out so loudly Sonnabend was startled and fixed his eyes on me.

"Well, no, actually. I think *you* may be okay."

Oh, thank God, thank God. Suddenly it made some sort of sense. I couldn't be dying at twenty-six—there was so much I wanted to accomplish. I wanted him to sign an affidavit. I wanted his sworn testimony that I'd be okay. I wanted a goddamn guarantee.

"But of course, you won't be all right if you go out and pick up more infections."

"That's why I disconnected my phones!" I was standing on two feet, but my soul had collapsed somewhere on the ground, overwhelmed with gratitude and glee. My life had just been yanked back from the abyss. "I don't care if I have to spend the rest of my life jerking off," I proudly proclaimed.

Sonnabend looked at me askance. I really meant it, but he wasn't buying it.

"But . . . don't I have the gay cancer?"

"Oh dear me, I see you've been reading. It's called AIDS and I would say you have a lesser or early form of it."

"But everyone with AIDS dies. I know—I called the Gay Men's Health Crisis hotline. I've read the *New York Native*."

"And so you believe everything you read and hear? How do they know that?" Sonnabend asked impatiently. "Look, this community—if you can call it that—is totally unprepared and unequipped to deal with this crisis. An enormous disaster is unfolding and all they want to do is throw theme parties to raise money, like it's something happening on the other side of the world and won't touch them. They hate me because I wrote an article in the *Native* saying that they have promoted a completely unhealthy lifestyle and now it's killing people."

"Because promiscuity is spreading the germ?" I asked.

"And what germ is that?" Sonnabend asked incredulously.

I was more incredulous that he was asking me. "I don't know, the AIDS germ, no?"

A weary look rearranged Sonnabend's face. "Not just a germ, it's probably many germs, many different viruses. It's very unhealthy to be repeatedly infected with hepatitises and syphilis

and parasites and cytomegalovirus and all these sexually transmitted diseases that are out there. You're intelligent. You know
that yourself."

I couldn't believe he was talking to me like I was supposed to
understand what was going on. AIDS was a brand-new, complex,
medical mystery that had doctors and scientists completely baffled,
but Sonnabend was telling me that I could draw on what I had
learned from my own experiences as a sexually active gay man in
New York City to figure some things out for myself. "But they told
me at GMHC that gay men who weren't promiscuous and who
were entirely monogamous are also dying of AIDS."

"I'm quite certain they love saying that," Sonnabend said, "because they can't or don't want to face the truth. If in fact a gay man
was monogamous and got AIDS, then you can bet his lover was
going out and picking up infections and bringing them home.
'Monogamous' doesn't necessarily mean mutually monogamous."

Boy, did that ring a familiar bell in this hustler's head. Many of
my clients had told me that they came to me because they were
"tops" (the active partner) in their relationships but needed to be a
"bottom" (the receptive partner) once in a while, too. I knew a lot
of lovers where the one who was the top in their relationship went
out to the baths and backrooms to be on the bottom. If I learned
anything from hustling it was that many men came to me because
they loved being a bottom—but didn't want anyone to know. Wow!
If men who loved getting fucked were part of the mystery of
AIDS, it might never be figured out. No one talks about anal sex in
public.

"But I don't understand why you sound so hostile to GMHC?
They're gay men, they're on our side, they're trying to help."

"Listen to me, if you want to live, you don't want them on
your side. They may think they're trying to help, but based on the
messages they're promoting and the experiences of my patients

who've had dealings with them, they're actually doing great harm. These people are amateurs—they have no background in the scientific areas that are relevant to this disease. These are life-and-death matters."

My adrenaline was racing from what Dr. Sonnabend was saying. He sounded like he knew what he was talking about, but I was hardly in a frame of mind to be skeptical of a man who had just yanked me out of a premature coffin. It was obvious that he was well educated. As I thought back on three years he'd been my doctor, I realized now in hindsight that he seemed to know something about everything and a lot about many things. I was bursting with questions about AIDS, and Dr. Sonnabend seemed like a gold mine of knowledge, a born teacher, provocative and passionate. Here he was taking time to educate me now that he could see my mind was open. He made me feel that whatever questions I had, all I had to do was ask, as long as I was prepared to feel stupid if my question was. "Are you saying that if you stop exposing yourself to all these sexually transmitted viruses and infections in time, a person can get better?"

"It's so much more complicated than that but, essentially, yes! Up to a certain point it's entirely possible that at the very least one might avoid getting sicker, maintain a certain level of health, and perhaps even get better. This is the message I'm trying to get out. Someone has to—it's terribly urgent. But there's no one to help me and I've got an office full of sick and dying patients. My first duty as a doctor must be to care for them."

I had to help him, and I knew how. "I just quit my, uh, job and I've got plenty of time if I can be useful. I can write, too. I majored in journalism in college. I've had plenty of articles published."

"I don't know if what needs to be done can be accomplished with the current leadership of the gay community. I fear they're befuddled by their self-importance and seem more concerned with protecting and promoting their image than with saving lives, and in light of what is going on now, that becomes almost criminal."

Anger began to swell inside me, but anger at my own beloved gay community? It's true: I couldn't actually define the term "gay community"—but I never let that alter the fact that I knew I belonged. Even recognizing that throughout the '70s gay men had little to do with lesbians and many gay men often treated each other badly, it was still a community, reflecting the best (celebrating diversity, fighting for progressive political change) and the worst (racism, sexism, ageism) of the dominant culture that produced it. I always knew that if I were fat, ugly, old, or handicapped, it wouldn't be so easy to feel so good about the "gay community." But I certainly believed that gays were part of a positive political force in America and that in some ways we were trying to move the human race forward even if we put that on hold to party. It was the gay liberation movement and the community it inspired that had helped me to learn to accept myself, which in turn made it possible for me to fall in love, have meaningful relationships, and develop a circle of gay male friends who expanded my definition of family. I felt those lessons could be a gift to the world, but most Americans weren't ready to hear it. No one ever encouraged me to go to the baths or hustle; that was my decision to keep letting my life be led by my dick. Surely, whatever feelings of anger at the gay community Sonnabend was provoking in me would simply have to be sorted out and redirected.

When we got back to his practice with our coffees, Dr. Sonnabend led me to his private office. He walked around the enormous piles of papers, journals, and books that surrounded his desk and filled my eager outstretched arms with scientific magazines, medical publications, and photocopies of AIDS research reports to read and return.

"Oh, and there's one more thing. I have another patient who is also interested in writing. Perhaps you should meet him."

"Perhaps? I must! Give me his name. What's his phone number?"

Sonnabend gave me his boilerplate perturbed "What-are-you-stupid?" look. "I can't do that without asking him first: patient confidentiality. I'll have to get his permission."

His permission? I couldn't understand why he was being so formal, but I knew this: After being his patient for three years, I was going to be learning a great deal more about him and what was happening. I raced home with my arms full of reading material, my heart unbelievably filled with hope, smiling from ear to ear with such joy and relief I was sure I looked like a certified idiot to the passersby, and I didn't give a shit.

As I sorted through the stacks of papers, arranging them in chronological order, I realized I had lost my Nina Simone record. Good riddance, I thought, enough with the woe-is-me, Greta Garbo act in *Camille*. Three days without a phone turned out to be a blessing. I had no idea of how to face death and now that my doctor said I wasn't dying, I was glad I didn't have to call back all my friends to explain a mistake like that. I grabbed a highlighting pen and a cigarette and I eagerly began to read.

⇐ ⇒

In the February 1981 issue of the *Journal of Infectious Diseases,* a report was published entitled "Prevalence of Cytomegalovirus Infection in Homosexual Men," written by W. Lawrence Drew et al. It documented a burgeoning epidemic of cytomegalovirus, or CMV, among sexually active gay men.

CMV is one of six different herpes viruses. It causes flu-like symptoms and, like other herpes viruses, can remain in your system for life after the initial infection. I assumed this was one of the "many germs" Sonnabend was referring to that might be contributing to the breakdown of gay men's immune systems. When I came down with hepatitis, my results showed I'd been recently infected with CMV, and I remember being shocked because I never even knew I had it. Now like a bolt of sober lightning, it struck me: How could I detect flu-like symptoms while partying for days and nights on end without sleep?

As I continued reading, it became clear that a lot of researchers were alarmed at the staggeringly high CMV infection rates among sexually active gay men.

In the December 10, 1981, issue of *The New England Journal of Medicine (NEJM)*, a group of doctors at UCLA reported,

> Several lines of evidence suggested that CMV infection was a major factor in the pathogenesis of the immuno-compromised state . . . 94% of exclusively homosexual men [studied] had serologic evidence of CMV infection. . . . It is therefore likely that sexually active young homosexual men are frequently re-infected through exposure to semen and urine of sexual partners. Such re-infection with large inocculum of virus before recovery . . . could conceivably lead to overwhelming chronic infection and immunodeficiency. . . .

A month later, in the January 28 issue of the *NEJM*, a "special report" appeared from the Centers for Disease Control (CDC), which stated, "CMV is often associated with P. carinii pneumonia."

The report cited extensive research published by Giraldo et al. between the years of 1972 and 1980 that "first suggested an association between Kaposi's sarcoma (KS) and CMV infection. . . . furthermore, CMV induces transient abnormalities in cellular immune function." Kaposi's sarcoma was the so-called gay cancer gay men were getting, but if it had a name, why did the *Native* ever call it gay? The report ended by noting that CMV infection was common in the United States and wondered how it might possibly account for the devastating immune deficiency seen in AIDS patients. This led them to consider whether the "widespread use of inhalants," amyl/butyl nitrites, better known as "poppers," which correlated with the large number of sexual partners reported among AIDS patients, might be playing a contributory role.

I did a quick mental inventory of my poppers usage. But the question that came to mind wasn't how much I'd done, but rather, if I could remember the last time I had an orgasm without them. But I rarely used them while hustling and it's not like I was one of those idiots sniffing poppers on the dance floor; that was really excessive.

In April 1982, *The American Journal of Medicine* reported the findings of a group of doctors working at Sloan-Kettering Cancer Center in New York City. They concluded, "We speculate that repeated and heavy exposure to CMV and long-term continuous antigenic stimulation . . . may result in secondary immune deficiency which may allow KS to develop further." Their conclusions on ten AIDS patients they studied noted, "similarities in the medical histories of these patients: six had received treatment for gonorrhea and four had been treated for syphilis at least once. . . . Three had also received treatment for amebiasis and two for giardiasis." Those were the parasites I'd had. "Four had acquired hepatitis."

They were all diseases I knew about firsthand, but I was determined to never get them again, so I guess I got out in time, as Sonnabend had said.

The next article was titled "T-Cell Ratios in Homosexuals" and to my surprise, Dr. Sonnabend was the lead author. It was brief, but it was published in a British medical journal, *The Lancet*. It featured a graph comparing the T-cell counts (one measure of the health of the immune system) of monogamous and "promiscuous" (defined as "more than 50 partners per year") gay men, and it showed promiscuous men had markedly weaker immune responses than monogamous men. It ended with a warning about promiscuity: "On the basis of these data, it would seem prudent for homosexual men to consider possible effects upon their immunological responses of the frequency and diversity of their sexual partners."

In June 1982, Arthur Levine, M.D., of the National Cancer Institute, published his findings in *Cancer Treatment Reports*. "It is clear that the syndrome is occurring mainly in a particular subset of the homosexual male population, possibly, but not exclusively defined by the number of sexual partners. . . . The median number of lifetime male sexual partners for homosexual male patients is 1,160. . . . Moreover, the number of bathhouse partners is increased in patients when compared to homosexuals who do not yet have the syndrome. . . . CMV is endemic in the homosexual male population, being sexually transmitted in the urine and semen." Levine argued that there must be some "new factor" to account for the appearance of this new syndrome, citing such possibilities as the use of "poppers" or that a retrovirus might be involved "as a consequence of intercourse with animals, thereby introducing it into the homosexual population."

The last comment on bestiality was typical of the ignorance and unabashed hostility toward homosexuality that was prevalent even in the highest levels of the medical profession. Dr. Levine and his publisher would never have been able to make such an offensive and speculative assertion about any other group!

In the June 1982 issue of the *Annals of Internal Medicine*, four reports and one editorial appeared. A group of researchers at the NYU Medical Center found that

> Our patients shared a number of distinctive character-
> istics: they were all young homosexual men, highly
> sexually active, with histories of many [STIs] and use
> of both prescription and recreational drugs. The re-

cent appearance of this disease may be associated with the changes that have occurred over the last 15 years in the lifestyle of homosexual men living in large urban centers. There has been a marked increase in gay bathhouses, bars and meeting places where multiple, anonymous sexual encounters occur. This has been reflected in the incidence of [STIs], not only syphilis and gonorrhea but also amebiasis, giardiasis, Epstein-Barr virus and CMV infections. Use of multiple recreational drugs, especially inhalation of amyl and butyl nitrites . . . is also an important aspect of this changing lifestyle.

Obviously, Sonnabend wasn't the only one looking at a more complicated picture of what was causing AIDS, and that reassured me he was on to something important.

Another article from the University of California School of Medicine in San Francisco concluded, "The lifestyle of these persons has changed in the last ten years leading to greater promiscuity and use of drugs. . . . Physicians will begin to see increasing numbers and forms of clinical disorders developing from impairment of immune regulation in this group of homosexual men."

I couldn't believe what I was reading—it seemed so clear—they were talking about the details and consequences of the fast-lane urban gay male lifestyle—my lifestyle. This lifestyle had been, and continued to be, celebrated and encouraged by gay writers and activists, some of whom were now leaders in the gay community's response to this epidemic. Just from reading these few reports, AIDS began to seem a lot less mysterious and more painfully clear. But already I could see danger in equating being gay with being promiscuous. Many of my gay male friends were in relationships, some open, some closed. Were they all going to pay a price for the

excessiveness and resulting ripple effect in microbiological consequences of a hardcore subset, smeared with the broad brushstroke
of anti-gay and anti-sexual agendas? With one glaring exception,
Levine's, these medical reports were, for the most part, not moral-
istic or judgmental or condemning, but rather necessarily objec-
tive. I had all the risk factors they wrote about, including CMV and
other STIs, going to bathhouses, the use of poppers and other
recreational drugs, and many, many partners. How could
Sonnabend say I'd be okay? Maybe he just didn't want to scare me.
My survival felt like it was on a seesaw.

While reading these articles, I kept skipping over the sections
describing the "case histories" of the patients the reports were based
upon because I kept seeing the word chemotherapy and I didn't
want to read about the side effects. But I was finally overcome by
curiosity and about what Sonnabend had said about using too much
chemo. This was no time to be squeamish; I went back and read
them all. Almost every single case history reported in grisly detail
how each patient was given high-dose chemotherapy and how it
consistently seemed to make patients sicker, causing other serious
medical problems to erupt, hastening their deaths. Gay men with
Kaposi's sarcoma, even those with just a few skin lesions, the purple
spots Nicky had, were given high-dose chemo and, soon after, the
Kaposi's disappeared but the patients soon all died from other, more
severe opportunistic infections. Their ages ranged from mid-twenties to late thirties. And all of these reports kept repeating the same
phrase, calling the cases they were seeing "only the tip of the iceberg"—a haunting image of what was unfolding.

I saved the few articles Sonnabend gave me that were not from
medical journals for last. I began with one he wrote, which had
been published only the week before in the August 1982 *New York
Native* titled "Promiscuity Is Bad for Your Health: AIDS and the
Question of an Infectious Agent." In it, Dr. Sonnabend argued that

it's a premature assumption that a single new killer virus could be the only way to account for AIDS. He warned that it was extremely dangerous "to publicly propose that any minority group carries a specific infectious agent capable of [spreading] severe immune deficiency and cancer.[el] While there can be no doubt that AIDS is a new phenomenon in gay men, this cannot be said with confidence about at least the Haitians or the IV drug users."

Promoting the view that AIDS was probably caused by some new killer virus was the Centers for Disease Control. They did one of the earliest and most influential studies (although it was of such poor scientific quality, it wouldn't be published for several years) in which they reported discovering a "cluster" of cases of AIDS among a small number of gay men in Los Angeles. They interpreted this to indicate that these men infected each other with an as yet unidentified virus. This was their proof that a new killer virus was spreading from person to person.

But, as Sonnabend argued in his article, this interpretation involves the assumption that all gay men are uniform with respect to the numbers and differences of their sexual partners. Recognizing the dangerous myth of the "homogenous homosexual," the absurd notion that gay men are the same (e.g. "promiscuous") and therefore all equally at risk for AIDS, Sonnabend pointed out that it was possible that the men who comprised the so-called contagion cluster might belong to "a rather small subsection of gay men with an unusually large number of different sexual partners." He explained that you could use the same reasoning to conclude that lead poisoning was infectious, if it was seen in a group of children who knew each other. In fact, the real significance of their knowing each other was that they played in the same lead-contaminated environment.

Sonnabend's article concluded, "The issue of promiscuity may well be central to this controversy. In connection with this, it should be stated that gay men have been poorly served by their medical attendants during the past ten years (and I include myself in this criticism)."

HIV had not yet been discovered, but Dr. Sonnabend had repeatedly emphasized that even if a new virus was responsible for this disease, promiscuity was no less an issue. As he said, "Germs may cause disease, but its people's behaviors that spread the germs."

No one knew there would be long-term consequences, but now Sonnabend was trying to move us forward into the reality of the new age of AIDS. As he concluded in his article,

> For years no clear and positive message about the dangers of promiscuity has emanated from those in whom gay men have entrusted their well-being. The message has been, rather, that responsibility consists of being screened for syphilis and gonorrhea every three months. This is what has been told to gay men whose health has continued to be undermined by repeated episodes of . . . so many [other] infections. The one outstanding risk [for developing AIDS] is multiple, anonymous sex, and by not vigorously warning our patients of the hazards of such activity, we have to some extent contributed to the genesis of the AID syndrome. . . . If we are to truly serve our patients, we must admit that our desire to be non-judgmental has interfered with our primary commitment [to our patients].

After reading that, I recalled the countless times Sonnabend had been telling me to "stop fucking around," and now for the first time, I fully understood why. I realized that I had begun to regard him as a nice but lowly clap-doctor to make it easier to *deflect* his repeated warnings and deny that something very dangerous was occurring. No one could have predicted AIDS would happen, and no one was to blame, but after reading what was being published in 1982 in the leading medical journals, there were no more excuses for continuing to put oneself and one's sexual partners at further risk. This was an urgent part of the message Sonnabend wanted help to put out.

Next I read the widely distributed *Gay Men's Health Crisis Newsletter* (Number 1, July 1982). Page one explained who they were:

> We are all volunteers concerned about a growing threat of diseases in our community. . . . Panic is now spreading among all of us. . . . GMHC hopes to give anyone who cares the essential facts about our health. We have no wish to scare or coerce anyone. We take no stand on the issue of sexual behavior. We have but one concern, the good health of gay men everywhere.
>
> As though the situation weren't confusing enough, our health emergency still seems to be shopping for a name. We chose AID (acquired immune deficiency), but there are others: GRID (for gay-related immune deficiency) and CAID for community acquired immune deficiency. The Centers for Disease Control prefers AIDS.

To my surprise, on page two GMHC launched into a strong defense of the unpublished CDC study on the LA cluster. This struck me as strange; with all there was to report, why would the "cluster" be the first thing they would choose to present in their newsletter?

I began to understand why, some pages later, when I read Marty Levine's essay, "Fearing Fear Itself." As Levine wrote,

> Where ever we gather—at our gyms, in bars, at parties—clone banter is switching from the four D's (disco,

drugs, dick and dish) to who is the latest victim. . . . The pages of our periodicals continuously harangue us with the latest medical research. . . . All this talk has produced a poisonous side effect. We are overcome by hysteria, afraid of the consequences to our health of the way we have been living. . . . The panic originates in the widespread belief that clonedom—that is, drugs and fast sex—causes the diseases. . . . Most gay men blindly accept the idea. . . . This panic lacerates our emotions. . . . many of us now regard our once-glamorous and exciting lifestyle as toxic. . . . We are left frightened, nervous and confused. We wonder what we have done to our bodies. Do all those years of frenzied drug orgies at the baths mean it is only a matter of time before we are stricken? We feel guilt over our past ways. We are obsessed about our health. A minor sore throat, a slight black and blue mark conjures up visions of pneumonia or cancer. We RUN to our doctors. . . . For some, this hysteria breeds self-hatred. The threat of disease and death erases more than a decade of gay pride. Internalized homophobia steps out of the closet as "homosexuality" is blamed for the illnesses. Terrified, we are staying horny. . . . It is becoming terribly declass to be ripped to the tits. . . . Giving up clonedom may cost us the gratification of key emotional needs.

I wasn't sure where Levine was going with this, but I was about to find out, and it would forever alter my blind gay patriotism. Levine concluded,

Sadly enough, all this hysteria and psychological disturbance is needless. The outbreak is far from an epidemic

> . . . and it is unlikely that the clone lifestyle alone can ex-
> plain what causes [AIDS]. . . . Only 292 (out of 373)
> cases of AIDS were among homosexual or bisexual
> men: 278 cases out of a possible 11 million [gay men]
> hardly constitutes an epidemic . . . the clone lifestyle
> theory does not hold water . . . especially among those
> men who are sexually celibate.

Now I started to comprehend the wrath of Dr. Sonnabend's
message and began to feel my own sense of anger. I mean, how
does a celibate gay man acquire AIDS? Was it transmitted by radio
tuning into gay men first? Was it falling from the sky only on gay
men? In his long meandering diatribe of denial, Levine captured for
all time the widespread denial of AIDS that would paralyze the response of the organized gay community through the crucial early
period of the epidemic and squander the lives of thousands of gay
men in my health situation who could have also survived.

It would take me years to admit that without the early influ-
ence of Sonnabend and his ideas about AIDS, I would have agreed
with everything Levine wrote only a few days before I read it. Now,
for the first time since coming out, I felt like a man without a country and a community, and hanging in the balance was my life and
the lives of tens of thousands of other gay men like me. This battle
I couldn't walk away from.

There's a lawyers' maxim that goes, "When the law is on your
side, argue the law; when the facts are on your side, argue the facts;
when neither is on your side, pound the table."

Levine continued pounding:

> Fallacious reasoning is the mark of the clone lifestyle
> theory. After taking detailed life histories from the earli-
> est victims, researchers found that many of them were

frequent drug users, were highly sexually active and had
recurrent bouts of venereal disease. But to suggest that
one causes the other is poor science. . . . Another flaw in
the theory is its failure to account for all those suffering
from these illnesses. Many of the gay patients report
being faithful to their lovers, entirely monogamous.

I wondered how many of them could have been lovers of
some of my clients.

When new ideas come along that are too painful to confront,
creating myths provides an escape route, a way to deflect what one
can't bear to face, in this case, the myths of the "sexually celibate"
and "entirely monogamous" gay men with AIDS. Although Levine
concludes by urging gay men to find emotional support, to be
more selective in choosing sexual partners, and even to consider
changing their lifestyle, he, like many activists who would follow,
didn't really want to face the possibility that the fast-lane urban gay
male lifestyle could itself contribute to the development of AIDS in
gay men.

The very last thing I had to read was an unpublished article
written in August 1981 by Dr. Sonnabend, titled "Immunosuppression, Opportunistic Infections and Kaposi's Sarcoma." It was his
earliest examination of the multiple factors that might play a role
in the development of AIDS in gay men. (A revised version of it
would appear in the May 1983 *Journal of the American Medical Association*.) In it, he didn't rule out the possibility that an as yet unrecog-
nized virus might also play a contributing role, but he argued that
many known immunosuppressive factors might be sufficient to account for AIDS and that these factors must be further explored.

With all my reading done, I now had a clear vision of a tidal
wave of suffering and death heading full force at the gay ghetto. We
were just at the "tip of the iceberg" with no end in sight. What I

had read refueled my fears for my own survival. I ached for some sense of certainty, but there was none yet to be found. How could a New York City hustler avoid becoming a victim of this plague?

The phone rang and I jumped. It was the phone company calling to tell me my service was back on with a new unlisted number.

I called Sonnabend to give it to him. He had already spoken to his other patient who wanted to write about AIDS. "His name is Michael Callen. He said you should call him as soon as possible at home or work."

Later, when I talked with Michael on the phone, he sounded so tired and weary, like he had seen it all and seen too much. We both agreed that Sonnabend's ideas were brilliant and offered a real foundation for some hope, and urgently needed to be presented to the community. Callen told me he was going to an AIDS support group meeting that night and urged me to come.

"I've never been to a support group," I said.

"Well prepare yourself for this one," said Callen. "Many of the guys are quite ill, taking chemo and some are still going to the baths."

"No!"

"Oh yes," said Callen. "You need to be invited by someone in the group in order to attend, so if you get there before me, just tell them you're my invited guest."

In our brief conversation, I felt a peculiar bond with him. I sensed that the weariness I detected in his voice was that he knew the horror that was in store for gay men. How much of that was first hand? After spending the day reading about all the suffering and death from AIDS, I was now going to see it face to face for myself.

"The Hustler, the 'Clap Doctor,' and the Bathhouse Slut"

Dr. Richard Sonnabend, Michael Callen, and the author, 1993

The support group meeting I was heading to was being held in the office of the St. Marks Health Clinic, a venereal disease clinic run by the gay community in New York City's East Village. As I walked there, my stomach began to churn with trepidation, so my mind took a soothing stroll down memory lane. I know it sounds strange, but this VD clinic was a place that held happy memories for me.

I had gone there several times in the late '70s to be tested for VD with my best friend, Rich. We'd smoke a joint on the streets walking there and make slut jokes while filling out our "Patient Sexual History" forms: "Excuse me, but my friend is going to need much more paper than this." The routine was to take a tube of blood to test for syphilis and some cotton swab cultures to detect gonorrhea. Secure in the belief that this took care of all the consequences of our sexual activity, Rich and I would race each other back to the bars on Christopher Street, where gay liberation was born, to go dancing, drinking, and cruising for more sex.

But that was before AIDS, when the notion that sex could kill was inconceivable to me. And now, on this sweltering August day in 1982, those happy memories couldn't soothe the utter dread I felt walking back to that clinic, this time to attend a meeting, New York City's first public support group for gay men dying of AIDS.

When I entered, there was a motley crew of gay men, about fifteen in all, sitting in a circle. I could see in their eyes that I was being sized up and checked out with that piercing sexual intensity gay ghetto "clones" were famous for. Is he hung? Top or bottom? Vanilla or S&M? I put up my actor's fourth wall, ignoring all of them until I had the chance to sit down and unwind.

But I couldn't relax. In the ten years since I'd come out, I too had come to see myself and other gay men as sexual commodities—and now, what could be less erotic and more revolting than being a gay man with the plague? I felt something familiar here that unnerved me: Just as with homosexuality a decade before, AIDS engendered the same feeling of bearing a stigma. In the thirteen years since Stonewall (1969) and the nine since accepting that I was gay (1973), homosexuality in the United States had been transformed from being a "mental disorder" to a "lifestyle," and now I feared it was about to be reclassified as a terminal diagnosis. I held on with all my might to Dr. Sonnabend's theory that I could regain my health by giving up promiscuity and allowing my immune system to recover, but the only thing I knew with certainty was that I didn't want to become one of these men.

I scanned the group as casually as I could, but I couldn't stop staring at Matthew. He was about twenty-three years old with such a sweet face and pretty eyes, I was momentarily blinded to the awful fact that he was completely bald from chemotherapy. Why did it always hurt me more to see someone who was good-looking suffer than someone I found sexually unattractive? It was a horrible thing to realize about myself as I looked at Matthew, but it didn't stop me from drawing imaginary thick brown hair over his honey-dew melon head. No wonder he was one of the sickest ones here. Who wouldn't have wanted to have sex with him?

Then there was Bob, who had these dizzying, bugged-out eyes, as if he had gone on one too many acid trips and never returned. He was wearing a black T-shirt with large white gothic letters that spelled "FUCK." How tasteless, I thought, to wear that in this setting. Or was it intended as a defiant political statement about sexual freedom even in the face of death?

No one would guess that Artie was gay—in speech he was pure, working-class Brooklyn. His delivery was loud, unfocused, meandering, and peppered with frequent pauses as if trying to recapture his train of thought or figure out what bullshit to manufacture next. As I wondered if he'd suffered brain damage from too many drugs, he boasted about being the proud inventor of the poppers gas mask. "No need to keep stopping and sniffing," he explained in classic American salesman-speak. He kept exchanging whispered comments with his close friend Tom, with whom, he said, he worked for the Pleasure Chest store chain designing dildoes, leather whips, and paddles—a craft they took obvious pride in. Tom mentioned a tattoo on his butt that said, "USDA PRIME," an exact copy of the government inspection logo that marked sides of beef. A lot of the men were still wearing the telltale keys dangling from the right side of their hips, the gay ghetto code for "bottom" or "I get fucked."

My initial feelings of dread deepened as I listened to their stories—gay horror stories, the same old anti-gay genre but with a vicious new twist. Here they were dying horrible, disfiguring deaths—yet what they talked about were their futile struggles to hide their barrage of illnesses; and if hearing that wasn't painful enough, how friends and family kept abandoning them when they inevitably found out they had AIDS. One man went home to Kentucky to tell his dad, who punched him in the face; he wasn't allowed to go home to die. Looking sick led many to be fired from their jobs, kicked out of their apartments, discarded by even their gay male friends who were terrified of being near the plague.

It was a creepy, gay déjà vu: Having to hide one's "illness" was the new gay closet; being fired, evicted, and abandoned when you were found "out" was a cruel, new verse of the same old song. Gay liberation had taken us one step out of the closet, and AIDS was shoving us two steps back inside.

There's a certain lifeless way a person's head tilts forward when the spirit inside them is broken, like a flower wilting, and the only view is down. I'd seen those drooping heads before in pictures of concentration camp victims. I recognized it here in the dispirited postures of the sickest men, and I realized I had seen it before in several of my hardcore S&M clients.

The men here talked about how terrifying it was trying to find medical treatments when even the doctors didn't know what was going on; few had health insurance or money saved to cover a medical catastrophe. And since the culture didn't value our lives, what reason did we have to hope that doctors and surgeons were any different? No one talked about living; the discussion revolved around how to face death while hiding what it was they were dying from the best they could. Any ray of hope would have disintegrated in all that gloom, so I clung even tighter to Sonnabend's ideas and my resolution to stop having promiscuous sex.

All this gay helplessness was sparking disturbing flashbacks in my mind from some of my S&M scenes, especially as I listened to them talk about having chemotherapy, like it was some kind of masochism scene they had to endure without question, an act of total submission. Some talked about their doctors like they were long-lost daddies—and you don't question what Daddy says—you just do what you're told like a good boy. "My doctor is so handsome," one man said and his face, ashen from chemo, suddenly lit up. I squirmed in my seat thinking, "He could be Dr. Death, but he's cute."

When Michael Callen began to speak, I knew it was him from the way he sounded during our introductory phone call. The clone inside me did an automatic assessment: total queen, burnt-out looks, too thin, nice hair. I smiled, and he smiled back without missing a beat in what he was saying. "I just want to welcome Richard here since I invited him and tell him a little about the group."

"We are an emotional support group for gay men with GRID, gay-related immune deficiency, or AIDS, Acquired Immune Deficiency Syndrome. We are not doctors or experts and we take no position on matters of treatment options, personal behavior, or individual medical decisions. We are here to support each other on whatever choices or decisions members make. Our group is modeled on Alcoholics Anonymous and we ask that what you see here and hear here remains here. Richard, would you like to speak?"

No, I thought, I'd like to kick you, as I realized everyone's eyes were now focused on me. I didn't want to say anything—I wanted to fling my arms into the air like Agnes Moorehead in *Bewitched* and disappear. All through the meeting I was like a rubber-necker on the highway morbidly mesmerized by the sight of a car crash; now that I had to talk, all I could do was look longingly at the red exit sign over the door, knowing it was too late to escape.

Unlike most of the guys here, I didn't look sick, just angry, and I could feel everyone eagerly waiting for me—the new butch on the block—to spill my guts. I thought back over the day, what Dr. Sonnabend had told me about the possibility of recovering from my immune deficiency, what I had read in the medical journals that supported his beliefs, and then I took a deep breath and tried to sort through a mess of emotions.

"I don't really have GRID—or is it AIDS?"

"Then what are you doing here, Dolly?" someone barked.

"Wait. Give him a chance," said another.

"I mean, I do have immune deficiency, persistent swollen glands, and I have been extremely promiscuous—"

Angry groans exploded in all directions as soon as the word "promiscuous" came out of my mouth. Their reaction was so virulent; it felt like they were all against me, like I was some kind of gay traitor. If I would have just shut my eyes and let my feelings surface, I would have broken down crying, but the anger I had held inside me since coming out kept me from expressing emotional pain or vulnerability to anyone outside my circle of friends. I began to sweat and chatter nervously as if surrounded by a pack of wolves, trying to keep them at bay.

"My doctor told me that I can get better and avoid progressing to full-blown AIDS if I stop fucking around and give my body a chance to heal from years of taking recreational drugs and getting sexually transmitted diseases."

Complete pandemonium erupted.

"You're *blaming* yourself!"

"He's so *guilt*-ridden."

"And in denial—it's one of the stages of dying."

"Miss Falwell has arrived. It's all our fault."

I had ignited a firestorm of outrage. I felt so defensive I couldn't stop fanning the flames. They were all embracing death, and they weren't going to take me with them. "You've all been talking about how much we don't know, how confused the doctors are, how all of this is new. Have any of you actually read the medical journals? I have, and what I read is that taking chemo when you already have a weakened immune system and multiple diseases is the worst thing you can do. The scientific journals are reporting what's going on with AIDS: bathhouses, sexually transmitted diseases, recreational drugs. I know that's why I'm here. I believe that's why I'm immune deficient. For me, facing that is my way to try and survive. If you read what I've read, you'd be as convinced as I am. My doctor thinks that I can get better and I don't know why the only thing you all feel sure of is that no one can. Pardon me for having a different opinion but I have little doubt that we got sick from promiscuity and all the infections we got and it makes sense that some of us might get better if we stop in time."

"Your doctor sounds like a real quack."

"You gotta call Gay Men's Health Crisis and get a good *gay* doctor."

"It's a virus that's making us sick—it's not our lifestyle!"

"She thinks she'll get better if she repents."

In a matter of seconds I had obliterated the polite serenity and order of the group, converting it from a wake to sheer chaos. Almost everyone began talking all at once while others just stared at me in disbelief and anger. They had been speaking about AIDS like it was a series of endless, unstoppable disasters, and now, I was one more to add to the list: a gay man who "blamed" himself for having the disease. I was afraid to even look at Callen. I worried that he'd be hated for inviting me and they all seemed to like him. I felt terrible about that. Mercifully, I had arrived late and the meeting was coming to an end.

"I'll see you Saturday night in the Saint balcony," I heard someone call to another, probably just to anger me—which it did.

"I'll see you there," another replied in a singsong trill.

As the men began to disperse, a professorial man stepped forward from the back of the room and introduced himself as the group facilitator. Pretending not to direct his comments at me, he said, "It's not our place here to judge others or to claim that any treatment, behavior or advice is preferable to any other. We're not doctors or experts. No one will be allowed to return if they are disruptive or upsetting the group members."

Yeah, I thought, have a good time fucking in the Saint balcony Saturday night and take some more gay men to the grave with you. Heavens, I wouldn't want to be judgmental or upset anyone for that. And as I thought about my friends, Rich, Joe, Rob going to the Saint on Saturday and ending up in the balcony with one of these guys, I couldn't wait to get home to warn them.

"Do you want to go for some coffee?" It was Callen looking at me with what seemed like sympathy and understanding. While a few of the men were telling the facilitator not to allow me back, Callen had the guts to come over and talk to me right in front of them.

"You don't hate me?" I asked in amazement.

"Quite the contrary, I agree with much of what you said and I'm glad someone finally said it. Cabbing from chemo to the baths and then bragging about it in the group—it's disgusting. But you have to realize that most of the men here are dying and they know it's too late for them to get better no matter what they do."

"Of course, you're right," I said, feeling like a complete idiot. "I have trouble dealing with death."

"Who doesn't? Our facilitator has apparently forgotten that's one of the issues this group is supposed to help people with. I think it was brave of you to say what you said. I can see that unlike most of the queens here, you're not ready to glamorize or embrace dying, and sick as I am, neither am I. But the closest people these guys have in their lives are all abandoning them when they need them most, and gruesome as this sounds, the baths are one of the few sanctuaries where they can still find human contact."

"It's all so awful—that never occurred to me. My friends are family, they'd never abandon me."

"I wouldn't know," said Callen. "I don't really have any friends."

He suggested cake and coffee at Rumbul's on Christopher Street. After our brief talk, I was ready to go anywhere he wanted, but I didn't know what stunned me more: that he was escorting me out amid plans to banish me from ever returning or that he was so open and honest about admitting something so pitiful that I couldn't imagine it—*no friends?* Make one up. Pretend. Or just nod your head in silence. When you're a gay man, what else is there? For most of us, dogs and lovers come and go, but our only hope of having a truly understanding family is by nurturing one with our friends.

Ten years later, Callen vividly recounted that moment as the first stark contrast between us. Neither of us, of course, had any idea as we reached the street and began walking that eight months later he would be giving a speech to the New York State Legislature that began his ascent to national prominence as one of the most effective AIDS activists, a co-founder of the people with AIDS (PWA) self-empowerment movement. He went on to give dozens of speeches around the country, testified before Congress, went to the White House, appeared numerous times on TV, sang an AIDS anthem he had co-written with Peter Allen on *Donahue* and *Good Morning America*, became an author, and was thanked by Tom Hanks at the Golden Globes for his involvement and appearance in *Philadelphia*. His legacy lives on in Manhattan's Michael Callen/Audre Lorde Community Health Center. At the end of that extraordinary journey, as Michael began to succumb to illness, it became important to him that someone remember who he had been before AIDS, when he worked as a paralegal and spent the rest of his time having anonymous sex, reading books, and being lonely. I remember. I became his friend that night; few things in my life have made me as proud.

When we reached Rumbuls, he picked a table by a window overlooking a garden, which was owned by one of my wealthier clients.

"What are you grinning about?" Callen inquired.

"Oh, nothing. Forget it," I said.

Callen stared at me intensely. "What did you do before AIDS? Did you work?"

I wasn't ready to answer, and I couldn't stop grinning.

"Okay," said Callen, "I'll start. I always have to go first to get gay men to open up. I've been a slut for ten years and I know that's why I'm sick. I like to say I am not just a bottom—I am *the* bottom. I estimate I've had approximately three thousand men up my butt and the only thing that's a mystery to me about AIDS is that I'm still standing on two feet. So tell me, queen to queen, what did you do for a living before AIDS?"

"I guess you could say I made a pretty good living making gay men happy."

"What does that mean? I tell you three thousand men fucked me and all you can say—"

"I was a hustler, but an S&M hustler."

"How S&M? It's such a broad term it's virtually useless."

"And you're a stickler for details."

"Am I ever. What was the one thing you did most or best, and be specific."

"Making them come with both holes filled."

"What were they doing when most of them did?"

"You mean like moaning or crying?"

"Uh huh . . . What else was there?"

"I never liked making them bleed."

Callen froze. I realized that had come out wrong. I was becoming Vinnie just from talking about hustling. One week into retirement and I missed him. Callen wasn't an easy queen to shock with his three thousand men, but from the look of him, I had succeeded. I was starting to worry about how to undo the damage done by what I'd said.

"See that garden railing by the tiny lights? I had a regular client who liked to worship me there usually around sunrise."

"Before or after the assault and battery?"

"You've completely gotten the wrong impression."

"Well if I did someone gave it to me."

"I never set out to make anyone bleed, I hated it, but I was doing what a client asked, which is how I learned. Would you believe I was just trying to make enough money to get back to grad school? I thought I could do it the way I worked my way through college, just getting blown."

"Why don't you start your story right there. What was wrong with a college loan?"

As I began to explain, Michael finally started to see who I was.

"I must confess," said Callen, "I've probably spoken to every hustler in *The Advocate*."

"Oh, you're one of those annoying callers who just wants to talk and keeps asking a million questions."

"C'est moi. I thought your voice sounded familiar. But I am not into that dreary, S&M spankin' butt crap. Just give me a hard fat dick, all the way in, all the way out. Are you a total top?"

"In S&M. Where did you grow up?"

"I was a small-town boy from Ohio: I think of myself as poor white trailer trash from the bowels of the Midwest. Growing up there was brutal for a sissy like me. Boys would come out of the shower after gym class, form a circle around me, and piss on me. I had the sense that if I told anyone about it they would say, 'You're sexually attracted to boys, so you deserve to be peed on.'

"When I went to college in Boston, I stumbled upon a busy men's room in the fine arts building on campus and to me, a country bumpkin, that was how gay men had sex. The sexual drive was so strong that after having sex in this public toilet I thought, 'I'm home. This is who I am and it's okay.'

"I began devouring feminist books to try to understand the roots of why sissies like me are robbed of our self-esteem. I felt such anger I wanted to dismantle patriarchy on the spot. I became arrogant and hostile, ready to do battle with anyone, starting with my devout Christian parents. Sex was how I discovered who I was, that I wasn't some freak of nature, that I wasn't all alone. I came to consider myself a lowly private on the front lines of sexual revolution. I thought we could change the world though sexual liberation and that we were taking part in a noble experiment: We were going to show straight America how silly they were being with all their sexual hang-ups. And then came AIDS, a cosmic kick in the ass.

"When I first moved to New York City after graduating from Boston University, I got hepatitis and a bad parasitic infection, shigellosis, having sex at the Christopher Street bookstore. At the time, I actually thought I had gotten sick eating at Kentucky Fried Chicken on 42nd Street. I even sued them and won. It truly didn't occur to me that what made me sick was licking a stranger's butt-hole in an adult bookstore booth. I was so ill, I had to drag myself to the Gay Men's Health Project in Sheridan Square and Dr. Sonnabend just happened to be one of the volunteer doctors on duty that night. He took one look at me and said, 'You're really sick— who's your doctor?' and I said, 'You are.'

"So it was completely accidental that he became my physician. I went to him over the years, but to me, he was just my clap doctor; we had no relationship. I kept inviting him to come hear me sing at clubs and cabarets. It was really hard for me to be assertive, to hand someone a flyer and ask them to come. Several times he said he would, but he never showed. I felt hurt, so I got a chip on my shoulder and I became a little cold and detached. Then, three months ago, I came down with cryptosporodiosis—"

"I read about that in the medical journals," I interrupted.

"What did it say?" asked Callen.

I remembered, but I didn't want to tell him, so why did I open my mouth?

"Tell me. I'm a truth junkie. I always want the brutal truth."

"It's a parasite . . . previously found only in livestock."

"No wonder I collapsed. I was hospitalized and I had a doctor who kept telling me there was no treatment and that I was going to die. When I didn't die and I got better, he seemed almost disappointed: My survival meant his mistake. He told me about a new AIDS support group and washed his hands of me. When I went back to Dr. Sonnabend, I was still pretty sick and while he was examining me, he got a phone call and left me in the examination room for like a half hour, so just to be a queen, I got up and started snooping around the room. There was something in his typewriter about his multifactorial model on the cause of AIDS and as I read it, all the problems about my health started making sense. His writing was so lucid and brilliant that reading it was absolutely life changing. It never occurred to me that all my sexually transmitted diseases could have cumulative consequences. When Joe returned from his call, I was bouncing off the ceiling, frantically telling him we had to get his ideas out to the community. When he said he had another patient who felt the same way, I begged him for your number, but he said he couldn't just give out patients' phone numbers and that he'd give you mine."

"Is cryptosporodiosis on that list of opportunistic infections that the Centers for Disease Control uses to classify an official AIDS case?"

"Yes, that's how I meet the CDC's definition of a case of AIDS, but I'm also an anomaly because everyone with AIDS who gets that infection dies from it." Callen became pensive staring out the window.

The look in his eyes gave me a chill; I knew he was at death's door, but this was the first moment I could actually feel it. I cringed at how callous I'd been in the support group. "I'm sorry, Michael.

My anger was misdirected at tonight's meeting. I wasn't thinking about you guys. I must have been quite a shock."

"My dear," Michael said with a smirk, "you were more like an electrocution, but you didn't understand what you had walked into and I like your fighting spirit. You know what I was just thinking? I hope when my time to die does come that I can face it without turning to God or religion because that would be a complete betrayal of everything I fought for and believed in."

The courage in those words took my breath away.

"The religious right rose to power on our backs," said Michael, "fundraising by scapegoating queers, and now this disease is going to give these bullies the biggest club yet to beat us all."

"I have visions of them dancing on our graves."

As we filled each other in about our lives, it became one of those rare conversations where instead of cutting each other off we stayed silent after each other's pause waiting to see if there was more. It was so clear that we could illustrate Sonnabend's theory, which suggested that multiple factors could be playing a role in the development of AIDS, which was so complicated, people kept calling it "a disease," when in fact, it was *a syndrome of diseases*. Searching for a single cause seemed to ensure the chances of missing the more complicated picture. Tens of thousands of people's lives hinged on finding out the cause(s) of AIDS; with more than 70 percent of all the reported cases being categorized as gay men, we had more at stake than anyone else. With our cockamamie belief that we could save the world, nothing could have stopped Callen or me in our quest to help wake gay men up, convince them that what was happening was real, and open their minds to taking a long hard look at how the way we lived our lives might have consequences on our health. We made a commitment, then and there, to begin writing an article explaining Sonnabend's immune system overload theory to the gay community.

"Two major sluts like us are just the ones to do it," said Michael.

By the time we left the café, I felt so close to him. Born the same year, we were both politically minded, unapologetic sluts eager to admit our mistakes, face the painful truths about AIDS, adapt, and fight—instead of lying down to die like doomed, compliant patients. Did he have any idea how much it meant to me to find someone who truly understood the magnitude of what was happening, someone who cared, who believed in himself enough to try and do something about it? We found each other caught on a beachhead, among the first to see the catastrophic storm that would soon be bearing down hardest on our little, isolated community. How could we get people to believe our warning that their lives were in danger when the media wasn't getting that news out, when there weren't even 400 cases of AIDS yet, when, historically, people don't want to hear bad news, let alone something that sounds like *The Invasion of the Body Snatchers*?

"I don't suppose I can convince you to come back to the support group," Michael said.

"I actually feel embarrassed and sorry now that I understand it better. But if we're going to fight this war, how can I stay away from what is the frontline."

"My point precisely. Don't come late again. No need to underscore the hostility from last time."

"I'll leave the bullwhip home."

"If only you could, my dear."

It was so easy to panic or become enraged, as I had in the support group. But as Michael and I parted on that oppressively humid night in Sheridan Square, where the story of our generation of gay men began at the Stonewall Bar, I knew I had found in him a calming thread of sanity.

❦   ❧

When I awoke the next morning, there was no way I could lie in bed with the gay world about to implode. I gathered my notes, photocopied articles, microcassette recorder, and headed to Dr. Sonnabend's office to wait for Michael.

"I see you two have met," Sonnabend said as he stepped into the waiting room. "How was the support group last night?"

Michael and I just shook our heads; we didn't know where to begin. This was the first time the three of us were together and there was so much strategy to plan for our writing, but Joe's waiting room was filled to capacity, and we would have to wait until he was done. By the time Joe got to see Michael, I was out of patience; I waited as long as I could, then I barged like a bull into the examination room and clicked on my tape recorder.

"They can try and pretend that this disease in gay men has nothing to do with promiscuity, but you'll see they won't get away with it for long," Dr. Sonnabend was telling Callen as I entered. "The community is at a critical point now; as people begin hearing what's going on they must be made aware that there is an alternative view to this killer-virus theory. Reasonable, alternative views must be out there for them to consider so at least they can keep an open mind."

"No one has even heard of your ideas," Michael said. "They make perfect sense to me as a slut and I'm sure they'll ring true for a lot of gay men once they have the chance to hear your theory."

"Or is that wishful thinking? So far all I've encountered is hostility for my *New York Native* article, 'Promiscuity Is Bad for Your Health.'[1] And if you look in the back of the Gay Men's Health Crisis (GMHC) newsletter,[2] there's a listing of what's been published thus far on AIDS," Dr. Sonnabend continued. "An article about poppers is referenced—but there's no mention of an article I coauthored on that same page in *The Lancet*[3] regarding my research on the association between promiscuity and immune deficiency. I can't prove it's intentional but it's hard to believe they missed it; it's fine if gay men disagree as long as they don't impede my research."

And it was true, when I looked, his article was missing.

Much as I hated facing the inescapable likelihood that my erotic rebel ways had a lot to do with my immune deficiency, there was a ray of sunshine. "I see a powerful element of hope in your theory, Joe, that as painful as it is to think we brought this upon ourselves—"

"Say 'unwittingly brought it on ourselves,'" Michael interjected.

"People can get better if they change their sexual behavior in time. We should use that as a selling point—right now we're at the tip of the iceberg—but we can curb this horrible disease," I continued. "There's no hope in what GMHC is saying, a killer virus is on the loose, and once you get it, you die. People just tune out hopelessness; that's what I was doing for the past eight months."

"But how are we going to break through gay men's vague awareness that something terrible is unfolding and the denial that it won't happen to them?" Michael asked.

And of course this was our main challenge—how to break through the fear and the conventional wisdom. Everyone was so scared that even though it was hard to ignore that something awful was unfolding, many were still keeping their heads buried in the sand—as I had.

"The way things are going, denial can't last long. When they see their sexual partners dying and start going to their doctors for checkups, they'll see for themselves what I've been seeing," Joe answered. "Fully three quarters of my patients already show some form of this disease."

"What are we going to tell them—to just stop having sex?" Michael asked Joe.

"No, you tell people that they have to find a few partners they know and trust. Sex is something one should reserve for people you care about and who care about you."

"I've heard about sex like that and it's no night at the baths," Michael said in devil's advocate mode, or was that pre-AIDS mode?

"Haven't you ever had a lover?" I was curious to know, with three thousand sampled. "That was the best sex I ever had."

"That's right," Joe agreed. "The more you grow to care for someone the better lovers you can become."

"It's true," I said, wondering suddenly how Rob was doing.

"Oh, *please,* you S&M hustler you," Michael exploded. "Who are you kidding?"

Dr. Sonnabend was incredulous and I felt exposed; it wasn't what I did that made me uncomfortable—it was people's distorted perceptions of what I might have done that gave me the willies. "Richard! You're a hustler? You like hitting people and giving pain?"

Just as I had dreaded. "It's not like that," I protested.

"Don't whitewash it, dear," Callen quipped. "Let's at least be honest with each other. You're just a nice Jewish boy with a bull-whip!"

At the time, I couldn't find the words to refute Michael's remark. I felt paralyzed. I'd encouraged it with what I said at the café. It's true, I had taken to S&M like a fish to water, but I was hardly the whip-wielding sadist he portrayed to Dr. Sonnabend. I may have been at the cutting edge of what was going on around me, but I wasn't alone. The ever increasing commercialization of urban gay male promiscuity produced a thriving underground industry of places where we could have anonymous sex with as many partners as we wanted. It turned my friends and me into kids in a candy store. The endless opportunities for ecstatic, anonymous sex seem to siphon off our collective anger, transforming angry activists into moaning, shopaholic sex consumers, hidden from public view in dark backrooms and bathhouse cubicles, exploiting each other like pieces of meat instead of treating each other like brothers. It felt so good on a physical level, who took the time to contemplate what it was doing to our bodies and souls? But now with the dawn of AIDS, I wondered, what more could a contemptuous America have asked for?

But on that day in Sonnabend's office when Callen called me a bullwhip-wielding sadist, I still felt safer wearing the mask of an S&M top than revealing the vulnerable, sensitive gay man so many of us were but so few of us seemed to want for sex.

"I'm sorry, Richard, I just assumed Joe was aware of your sex life," Michael said. "Personally, I'm so sick of being sick I don't even care about sex anymore."

"If you wish to write, you better care," Dr. Sonnabend retorted. "You must celebrate gay sex in your writing and give men support, but point out that right now there are certain activities that have simply become too hazardous at this time. Michael, just because you've gone through men like a box of used tissues—"

"I admit it! I thrived in these dark, dingy backrooms where people were on drugs and had low self-esteem because I thought I was just a big old queen, that I was unattractive and nobody would want me."

"I think what attracted me most about the baths was that there were always so many hot and more experienced men who wanted to have sex with me and they took me to heights of pleasure I had never known," I added. "I loved being able to compartmentalize my being on the bottom from the rest of my life where being my own boss and being masculine brought me so much adoration and reward."

"Maybe there are limits to promiscuity; maybe the body can interact with more people than one's spirit can," Dr. Sonnabend said. "We have departed from something that historically people must have learned without understanding how it came about. Culture has evolved certain social pressures toward a bond or a kind of responsibility among people who become sexual partners, ideas shaped over hundreds of years. I'm quite sure that when people were promiscuous in the past, infections occurred, even if just with syphilis and gonorrhea, and people got sick or died. Perhaps there is kind of a faded, cultural memory of this."

"Well, maybe not that faded: I can hear the whole country chanting a chorus of, 'We told you so, you fags,'" Michael said.

Now there was an obstacle to getting our message out if I ever heard one.

"But when one compares the dangers inherent in this message with saying that 'gay men,' implying all gay men, are spreading a killer virus, that creates the more dangerous scenario," Joe said. "Gay men are already dying and so many more will continue getting sick until we know the truth and face it. Most gay men don't run around at the baths or screw everyone in sight. Why should they be made to suffer by those who did? Read what you've copied and please take this writing seriously. I'm counting on you both. Someone has got to try and alert gay men to what's happening and that we don't know what's causing it. Do you realize what danger lies in this killer-virus theory? It's insane for GMHC to be whole-heartedly endorsing the Centers for Disease Control—the government that doesn't give a damn about them—and promoting this theory as fact when it's still unproven. Can't these fools see what lies down the path they're taking? Quarantine, panic, the worst kinds of discrimination for a group that doesn't even have basic civil rights. I believe the men at GMHC don't want anyone to see what goes on in the bathhouses and backroom bars. Believe me, the CDC doesn't want to look at it either. And so together, they embrace this simplistic theory which will bring perilous consequences and divert us from the hard work of trying to fully understand this disease."

According to Artie and Tom in the support group, the co-workers from the Pleasure Chest adult store, there was an interesting fact about the current focus of research that the CDC was doing but that no one talked about, which illuminates Dr. Sonnabend's point. The CDC was studying a group of men who had sex with each other and all came down with AIDS. As GMHC explained it in their newsletter, "The upshot of this information is that one or more infectious agents—germs, microbes, viruses, bacteria—were most likely passed through sexual contact from one gay man to another" (p. 12). The CDC was talking about this cluster as evidence of an infectious agent being transmitted from one man to another. But no one mentioned what Tom and Artie knew: This cluster being used as evidence of a new sexually transmitted agent comprised various members of a sex club who may have well been exposed to a lot of other agents, too: they were the members of the Fist Fuckers of America, L.A.; several were former friends and sex partners of Artie. In an age before safe sex and condom use was the rule, it's quite likely that these men were exposed to more than just a new virus, such as the many common sexually transmitted viruses that had reached epidemic proportions during the 1970s. The CDC never mentioned that in its *New York Times* interviews. But neither did GMHC.

As I walked Michael home, he said, "Joe's a brilliant scientist with a good heart, even though as a doctor, he has a completely unorthodox bedside manner. He may seem eccentric at times, but when you listen to him talk, peek beneath the surface and you'll see, it's the eccentricity of genius."

"You just captured him," I said. "I guess when you're as highly educated as he is, and you refuse to sell out to the system, it can make you seem a little off track because you live in a mediocre world that's run by idiots."

Dr. Sonnabend had been my doctor for over three years but I didn't know much about him. Michael was quick to start filling me in.

Joe's parents were highly educated, Jewish, European liberal socialists. They must have sensed what was coming for the Jews in

Europe because in the early 1930s they fled to South Africa, where Joe was born. His father was a noted intellectual and a professor and his mother and her sister were both physicians in private practice—an extraordinary achievement for women in the early 1930s. They provided Joe with an intellectually fertile upbringing.

He became a member of the prestigious Royal College of Physicians of Edinburgh and worked as a laboratory virologist in the 1950s with Alick Isaacs, the man who discovered interferon, a class of proteins released by cells invaded by viruses. Joe made important contributions to the scientific understanding of how interferon works. While snooping around the doctor's office that fateful day he was made to wait while Joe took a call, Michael discovered stacks of Sonnabend's published research spanning decades.

When AIDS was first reported in 1981, Sonnabend realized his patients—mostly gay men since his office was in the West Village— were an invaluable research resource. Most of his professional life was spent doing microbiological research on interferon-related studies, so he contacted laboratory friends and colleagues and started research collaborations with them. Before coming to his private practice each morning, he worked at a research lab at New York University. He was also busy collecting and sending blood samples of his patients to Stuart Schlossman, a Harvard immunologist, and Robert Friedman at the National Institutes of Health in Bethesda, trying to understand what was going on in AIDS. Schlossman was one of two people who developed the technology we use today to identify T-cell subsets and AIDS was first defined as a disorder of T-cell subsets using this technology.

In addition to all this, Joe was also spending a lot of time writing about his findings and theories. He wasn't being paid for any of this work and it was incurring additional expenses while cutting down on the number of patients he had time to see. Money was getting so tight he was considering a suggestion of one of his patients to establish a nonprofit foundation to support his research activities.[4]

"I never knew any of that," I told Michael. "You really know how to get a person's story."

"I do, don't I?"

It was an extraordinary realization: Dr. Sonnabend was a research scientist whose decision to work as a doctor in the late 1970s before AIDS began placed him on the cusp of research and patient care with expertise that could address both needs. And if that wasn't enough of a perfect fit, he had chosen years before to specialize in treating sexually transmitted diseases. Safe sex couldn't have asked for a better inventor.

In the ensuing weeks, Michael and I got together to write every time he had a spare moment and an ounce of energy: he was suffering from chronic mono and working full time as a paralegal, which made it difficult to find time for writing. The basic concept of our article was Michael's idea. We were going to call it "We Know Who We Are" and write it in the graphic language of the street, or as Michael said, "queen to queen, slut to slut."

"We're gonna turn up the lights and rip off the cubicle doors," Michael said. "Whoever reads our article may hate what we say, but they're going to know they've cruised the same paths, fucked at the same places and possibly had sex with one of us. They're going to know AIDS happened to us and it's going to happen to them."

"We may not feel comfortable talking openly about promiscuity and anonymous sex," I added, "but we know who we are."

I began spending my days in Joe's office. He was doing extensive blood, viral exposure, and immune system testing on more and more patients, including me. I wanted to understand what all the different blood test results meant because they gave a partial picture of the immune system. Before AIDS, patients had to wait a long time to get to see Joe for their appointment, but once you got to him, he gave you all the time you needed, which was great, un-less you were the next patient waiting. Now, with all the new test-ing, it was slowing Joe down even further. Plus, more and more young men kept showing up in a panic. One hectic day, Joe asked me to help out by explaining what the tests meant to patients, "but not with their actual results," explained Joe, "that's confidential."

So, I taught his patients using copies of my own results; teach-ing them educated me. In addition, whatever new research was being published about AIDS in medical journals arrived daily in Joe's heap of mail. I couldn't have chosen a better human labora-tory to learn about this disease than the office of a large gay prac-tice in the heart of the gay ghetto.

When Michael and I wrote together, I sat on his fire escape looking out on the city skyline, thinking of all the gay men who were still out there having anonymous sex with unknown partners, unaware of the deadly risks they were taking. There were occa-sional stories on the news by this time, and a well-attended forum held by Gay Men's Health Crisis, but nothing conveyed the gravity of what was unfolding to enough people; the media coverage was still sporadic at best, and most gay men, like most Americans, were still in the dark. I knew they'd be scared shitless if they saw what I was seeing each day in Dr. Sonnabend's office.

One day when I arrived at his practice, Joe looked particularly grim. "Do you remember that man I introduced you to last night?"

"How can I forget? He's so gorgeous."

"He went home and committed suicide. Please come with me. I have to go identify his body."

I made a lame excuse to get out of going. I wasn't ready for dead bodies. What I was witnessing on a typical day in the office was quite enough. The most common opportunistic infection that seemed to target mainly gay men was a cancer called Kaposi's sar-coma (KS). It produced purple lesions all over the body, but the real fear was that if they were also spreading internally, death could come quickly. In a few cases, KS was particularly aggressive and it could make a person's head swell to unimaginably monstrous proportions. One such patient was featured on a TV news special hosted by Geraldo Rivera; the image of the patient's bloated head covered with lesions all over his face and eyes and ears catapulted those who saw it into a state of panic. Few had rarely seen such a disfiguring disease, and to drive the horror home, a picture of the handsome patient before AIDS was shown. After that, droves of gay men were showing up in Sonnabend's office in a panic over every black and blue mark or mole. Others came in with shingles (herpes zoster), an often virulent reactivation of chicken pox that would appear as a swath of painful open sores spreading across the torso or the face. If it broke out across the eyes, you could be left blind, if it got into your spinal fluid, you could become paralyzed and if it traveled into the brain, you were left in a permanent vegetative state. But the one opportunistic infection that seemed to kill the quickest was pneumocystis carinii pneumonia. When a person was suspected of having it, he had to undergo a grueling procedure where miniature scissors were plunged down the esophagus so pieces of lung tissue could be cut off for testing. Michael had given me all the gory details of what it was like when he had that procedure. Harder to measure and quantify was the absolute terror of so many of the gay men calling and coming to Sonnabend's office. And with each passing day, the office became more crowded and the panic of gay men kept escalating.

On many nights Joe wasn't done seeing patients till well past 9 P.M. and sometimes I would accompany him as he raced around the city to check on his patients in hospitals. One night we visited a man who was angrily refusing a life-support machine that required a thick tube down his throat to artificially keep him breathing. But he had no living will—who in their twenties thought of such things?—and when we returned the next day he was under heavy sedation and, just as he had feared, the tube had been run through a surgical cut in his cheek against his will. He was kept alive for weeks but never woke up again.

For someone like me who had gone through life with a neurotic fear of surgery and medical procedures, this was my worst nightmare, but it felt bearable because Sonnabend kept assuring me I'd be okay. What I didn't realize was the psychic toll, trying to cope with the depth of gratitude I felt from realizing I'd been saved from all this horror in the nick of time. Many nights I couldn't fall asleep; some mornings I'd wake up thinking it was all a bad dream.

Panic over the fear of contagion began spreading throughout the city. AIDS patients were being shunned and mistreated everywhere they went. Hospital workers were afraid to walk into their rooms and threatened to strike if they were forced. Food trays were left on the floor outside patients' doors. Dentists began turning away AIDS patients; morticians began refusing to embalm the bodies. Television film crews were being paid an additional fee for "combat duty" to photograph interviews with AIDS patients; one technician threw a microphone to Callen from across the room and asked him to pin it on himself. Fear and panic kept escalating to the point where any man even suspected of being gay was regarded as a likely carrier of the emerging deadly plague. Stories of "single men" committing suicide, sometimes leaping from windows of high-rise buildings, were frequently reported ambiguously on the news. Friends would call me, wondering if the impetus had been AIDS; several times we found out through the gay grapevine it had.

After nearly two months of writing, I was out of patience with Michael's endless rewrites and I exploded. "Come on, let's get this out already!"

"I completely understand your impatience, but do you realize what it is we're doing? We're about to dismantle an entire subculture and we have to anticipate their attacks. If we're not careful, if our arguments aren't completely airtight, they'll destroy us. They'll shut us right out of community debate."

"I can't take it anymore, Michael. It's gone from three hundred to over six hundred cases and we're still polishing our first article. Let's take it to Joe and see what he thinks."

⇜   ⇝

Dr. Sonnabend wasn't pleased. "You keep overstating the scientific implications of the multifactorial theory. What I am suggesting is a theoretical model, a conceptual framework. These ideas have to be tested in a laboratory before one can say they're true."

We wanted to challenge the people who had jumped on the killer virus theory bandwagon, but Dr. Sonnabend warned us not to repeat their mistakes by becoming zealots for an alternative view. I heard what he was saying but I was too emotional about what was happening to rein myself in; friends said that when I argued Dr. Sonnabend's views about AIDS, I was like "Vanessa Redgrave crashing on a bad acid trip." I had no patience for the cautionary approach of science.

"We have no scientific basis to dismiss the chance that AIDS is caused by a single virus; we must leave that possibility open," Dr. Sonnabend warned. "We're all on new territory with this disease and we better respect that fact even if others don't. One should go through their statements and refute what they are saying point by point."

I kept emphasizing that what we were writing was not a medical report but instead a call to arms. Looking back, I realize this was naïve, but the emotion and fear of the times crowded out rationality. Dr. Sonnabend made me feel as if he had yanked me out of a coffin in the nick of time; I kept panicking about my friends and all the other gay men who, with each passing day, might be losing that chance to save their lives. Be patient? Not a chance.

Joe had begun sharing his office space with a young black doctor named Terry. As Michael and I were leaving, he stopped us. "Joe told me about the writing project you're both working on. I think what you're doing is important. If I can help in any way, don't hesitate to ask."

"Here's a copy of what we've done," said Michael, "but it's just a draft."

Terry belonged to a gay, black professional group that held monthly socials. They had invited him to speak about AIDS. After reading our article, he called Michael and asked him to take his place. Terry indicated that there would be over 300 gay men there as well as representatives from the GMHC. It was a perfect opportunity to test the waters with our message, and Michael, a professional singer, had no difficulty speaking in front of a large audience.

The night of the meeting, with tape recorder in hand, I met Michael outside the auditorium of the Martin Luther King High School. We had put into Michael's speech some of the vitriol Joe had edited out of "We Know Who We Are." We were nervous about that, but Michael looked relaxed as we entered the auditorium—or was it just pure exhaustion?

After several complicated medical presentations few could understand and what came off like a happy sales pitch from GMHC President Paul Popham, Terry introduced Michael.

He looked so gaunt as he walked to the podium to speak, and I could feel anxiety filling the auditorium as people finally got a look at the real thing—their worst nightmare—a gay man with the plague.

"You've just heard a lot of facts and statistics and it all sounds pretty depressing. But with all due respect to the doctors here, what has been missing from most discussions of the present health crisis are the experiences and opinions of those of us who have unwittingly created it. The question on every concerned gay man's mind is, am *I* at risk for AIDS?

"I am a gay man with AIDS and I have been asked to speak to you tonight about my experiences. No intelligent discussion of AIDS can occur until one understands just how AIDS is developing in gay men. Understanding the correct theory of what causes AIDS is critical because each theory has different ramifications for treatment and prevention.

"Unfortunately there is a popular theory which holds that AIDS in gay men is caused by some new, mutant, killer virus, and that a single sexual contact with me could infect you with AIDS and kill you. This theory, endorsed prematurely, in my view, by the CDC and most gay doctors who treat sexually active gay men, proposes that gay sex has become a game of Russian roulette with some unidentified killer virus as the bullet. I don't plan to spend much time refuting this unsupported science fiction. Rather, I want to suggest that AIDS in gay men is caused by re-exposure and reinfection with common viruses and infections which are presently epidemic on the urban gay circuit of backroom bars, bathhouses, adult bookstores, and tearooms.

"Can anyone deny that hepatitis A and B, syphilis, gonorrhea, herpes simplex types one and two, intestinal parasites and many common viruses like cytomegalovirus not previously considered venereal are now epidemic on the urban gay circuit in 1982? I'm sure the CDC is well aware of this. What I want to suggest is that AIDS does not spread in the classic sense of contagion, but rather, it develops over time. The sexual histories of every gay man with AIDS I have met have been consistent with mine. As the National Cancer Institute reported this year, 'The median number of lifetime sexual partners for gay AIDS victims being studied is 1,160.'

"One thousand, one hundred and sixty! That number indicates a very specific lifestyle. Of course not all of us tell the truth about the extent of our sexual behavior, especially to some heterosexual government interviewer from the CDC, so let me relate my own experience as directly as I can.

"I am twenty-seven years old. I've been having gay sex in tearooms, bathhouses, bookstores, backrooms and adult movie theaters since I came out at seventeen. I estimate conservatively that I have had sex with over three thousand different partners. I arrived at this figure by taking a long, hard look at the patterns of my sexual activity—something I advise every concerned gay man to do. I estimate that I went to the baths at least once a week, sometimes twice, and that each time I went I had a minimum of four partners and a maximum of, well, let's just use four.

As Michael looked at me and smirked the auditorium filled with nervous laughter.

"But let's not count this last year because I have stopped promiscuity entirely. So that's nine years of active promiscuity, fifty-two weeks in a year, times four people a week, is 280 different partners a year. Times nine years equals 1,872 different sexual partners. And that's just the baths!"

A hush came over the crowd.

"I also racked up about three men a week for five years at the Christopher Street bookstore, so that's another 580 men. 1,872 plus 580 is 2,452. Then, of course, there was the Mine Shaft; the orgies; the 55th Street Playhouse; the International Stud backroom; trips to similar establishments in San Francisco, Los Angeles, Atlanta, Boston, and Europe. You see my point.

"But the issue with AIDS is not so much the number of sexual partners as it is the corresponding history of sexually transmitted diseases. Let me present my own history of STDs.

"From 1973, when I came out, to 1975, I only got mononucleosis and nonspecific urethritis, or, NSU. In 1975 I got my first case of gonorrhea. Not bad, I thought. I'd had maybe two hundred different partners and I'd only gotten the clap twice. But then, moving from Boston to New York City, it all began to snowball. First came hepatitis A in '76 and more gonorrhea and NSU. In 1977, I was diagnosed with amebiasis, an intestinal parasite, hepatitis B, more gonorrhea, and NSU. In 1978, more amebiasis and my first case of shigella, and of course, more gonorrhea. Then in 1979, hepatitis yet a third time, this time type non-A, non-B, more intestinal parasites, adding giardia this time, and an anal fissure as well as my first case of syphilis. In 1980, the usual gonorrhea, shigella twice, and more amebiasis. By 1981, I got some combination of STDs each and every time I had sex, and I finally contracted herpes. Last June I was hospitalized with a diagnosis of cryptosporodiosis, described in the medical journals as 'a disease common in livestock.'

"At age twenty-seven I've had: gonorrhea, syphilis, hepatitis A, hepatitis B and hepatitis non-A, non-B; intestinal parasites including, amebiasis, e.histolitica, shigella, giardia; herpes simplex types one and two; venereal warts, mononucleosis, cytomegalovirus, and now cryptosporodiosis, for which there is no known cure. And this does not include the many colds, flus, sore throats, rashes, and other infections, which at the time I did not connect to my sexual activity.

"I believe there are many different pathways to AIDS. I believe I have just walked you down mine."

Michael paused to look out to the audience. He wasn't trying to blame gay men—he was trying to illustrate how much it took for him to reach a point where he had no choice but to change his sexual behavior and take responsibility.

"Let me assure you: I have no problem with being gay or with having a lot of sex. I have problems with diseases that resulted from my promiscuity. I am simply sick of being sick.

"Now, I have tried to be a 'good gay' and, as one gay author suggested in a course I took at the New School,[5] and I quote: 'To wear my sexually transmitted diseases like red badges of courage in a war against a sex-negative society.' But now the stakes are too high. Gay men are dying and a new case of AIDS is being reported every day. Surely it's time for a rational re-evaluation of the promiscuity we hold so dear. Shall we blindly defend promiscuity literally with our lives? These are hard and difficult questions, which we as individuals and as a community will have to grapple with if we are to survive into the '90s.

"In the end, no one should try to legislate health risks. I have never and will never suggest such a thing. But what is required in this crisis are clear and unequivocal warnings about the health hazards of the promiscuous urban gay male lifestyle. And even if there is a new virus found and implicated in the cause of AIDS, promiscuity is the way it's being spread.

"I'm aware that what I am saying about promiscuity raises a lot of difficult questions for sexually active gay men, but just because something is difficult doesn't mean it isn't necessary—and for some of us—vital.

"And there is some good news in all of this suffering and despair. Currently the life expectancy of a gay man diagnosed with AIDS is a mere sixteen months. But since I stopped promiscuity, my health and blood test results seem to be holding steady. I've learned to listen to my body, to sleep when I'm tired, reduce stress, eat a more healthful diet, and avoid placing any more burdens on my health. From what I've seen in my support group for gay men with AIDS, one reason many gay men may be dying so quickly is that they continue living in the fast lane of recreational drugs and multiple sexual partners, which makes picking up more viruses and infections inevitable. They may see no hope, but I refuse to live without it. I refuse to die on cue no matter what the experts' predictions say. I plan to fight and survive this disease for as long as I can.

"We are told that out of every tragedy some good comes if only one can see it and seize it. AIDS provides us with the unique opportunity to begin a long-overdue rational discussion about the role of promiscuity in defining gay maleness. This dialogue must begin now, for surely, it is a matter of life—and death."

In an instant, every single person in that auditorium shot out of his seat to applaud. It was deafening. Michael's first speech convinced me that he was well on his way to becoming an effective and persuasive spokesperson for people with AIDS.

Through August and September, our AIDS support group meetings were filled with nothing but stories of misery, despair, and modern medicine's well-intentioned butchery. Matthew, for example, was being pressured by his doctor to have an experimental chemotherapy spigot implanted through his skull and left there for ongoing treatments. New people would show up, hear stories like that, and not return, but as painful as it was listening to these experiences, it could be even more unbearable trying to face AIDS alone. And so, by November 1982, attendance had doubled from fifteen: the sheer explosive growth of the epidemic ensured that more and more men would fall ill and seek support from their peers.

We were forced to move to a larger space—the office of the National Gay & Lesbian Task Force (NGLTF) on lower Fifth Avenue. The first time Michael and I went there, we were so disillusioned to see that America's leading national gay organization fighting for our civil rights looked so small and cramped and was barely surviving financially. As I surveyed the piles of papers on every desk, I realized that the staff was overwhelmed with work and ill prepared to muster the resources needed to confront a new disaster. Seeing this room revealed to me the awful vulnerability of queers in America at the dawn of AIDS.

The support group sat in a circle in the center of the office while all around us NGLTF volunteers manned hotline phones, giving out information, or counseling callers who felt tormented about their homosexuality. We could tell by the comments of the counselors hovering over phones that a few callers were suicidal; others had been taunted or beaten just for being perceived as gay; and some only wanted directions to the nearest gay bar. Our attention kept moving back and forth from the talk within our beleaguered group to the words of the crisis counselors, an emotionally jarring juxtaposition. The acronym AIDS was barely five months old and America's bullies had yet to learn it, but we knew sitting here that AIDS would soon be causing more gay suffering and death than all the suicides and anti-gay violence combined.

Michael had noticed that whenever he could find the right moment to turn the topic of discussion to sex before AIDS, even the sickest among us lightened up, some smiling and even laughing for the first time; many couldn't resist sharing stories about the glory days. Michael always had to go first, breaking the ice with his own graphic confessions before anyone else would open up, but once he did, the floodgates unlocked. We desperately needed a break from the endless horror stories each new member brought with him, and talking about sex before AIDS was like getting high, a way to let off some steam.

After my explosive first meeting, I had decided to lie low and let Michael do the talking. With his midwestern sincerity and gay wit, he had a knack for pulling the most intimate sexual details out of the shyest people, often turning to me and whispering, "I'm so shameless." Everyone kept saying that Michael should have worked for the Centers for Disease Control, which was sending epidemiologists to the hospital bedsides of the earliest gay men with AIDS to interview them for a research study on the risk factors for acquiring the disease. Some patients had refused to cooperate. Artie loved telling us how he'd made a conservative government epidemiologist queasy as he matter-of-factly explained that dildoes and fistfucking were often the only ways he could fuck at the baths because "Who could keep their dicks hard with all the drugs we were taking?"

"I guess I went off on a long tangent about how that led me to discover my love of rimming," Artie explained, "when finally he interrupted me to ask what rimming was. When I told him, he excused himself and went running to the bathroom clutching his questionnaires. I guess it upset him—but he asked!"

What Michael and I experienced in the support group meetings fueled and shaped what we were writing for our article. We were arguing that the party was over and that promiscuous gay men like us had to just stop having anonymous and promiscuous sex, either to safeguard their health or to give their immune systems time to heal. Then, at one meeting, Phil Lanzarratta, New York's first publicly identified gay man with AIDS, who wrote a seminal cover story about living (as opposed to dying) with AIDS for *Christopher Street* magazine[6] talked about still going to the baths. Michael asked him, "Aren't you worried you might give someone this disease?"

Phil replied, "No, everyone knows sexually transmitted diseases are out there and that we're taking our chances when we go out. They probably all have it anyway; one of them gave it to me. It's every man for himself."

After the meeting I told Michael, "What Phil said was so coldblooded I could see the disgust in your face."

"No," Michael responded sadly, "what you noticed was something worse. Something resonated inside me as I listened to Phil, a voice that kept saying, 'That's me talking!' Put your emotions and outrage aside for a moment and just look at Phil. He's gentle, sincere and honest, he wouldn't want to hurt a fly. He's like a lot of queens, and he's like us, too. It's my theory that Phil is partly a consequence of something that happened in the late '70s with the epidemic of intestinal parasites. Everyone was getting infected, and there were all these articles about it in the gay press. But unlike gonorrhea or syphilis, you couldn't just take a few pills or get a shot and go back to the baths in a few days. With parasites, treatment took over a month, and few were willing to give up sex for that long. That was the first ethical compromise on a wide scale among us sluts where we justified having sex when we knew we were sick. I did it and you did it. For gay men who thought nothing of going to their clap doctors for antibiotics before they went to the baths, parasites presented an ethical obstacle we were unwilling to let get in our way. I also think many of us were becoming numb to sexually transmitted diseases, in part, because we thought that there would always be a pill or shot for anything we got.

"I remember one Friday night when I was shitting my brains out and feeling angry because I always went to the baths on Friday night. I was going to there to get fucked—there was no other reason—and I remember this image of myself sitting on the toilet checking my watch and thinking, 'Hurry up, when is this shit gonna stop? I gotta go.' I wasn't thinking, 'I'm sick. I should rest. Maybe I have the flu or amebiasis again.' When it came to getting fucked I wasn't concerned with my own health, so how could I be concerned with someone else's?

"What I'm saying, Richard, is that when we react to Phil, we have to recognize a degree of him in ourselves. We have stopped being promiscuous and we're arguing in our article that gay men like us should too, but I just don't know how we're going to shape this message for the sister sluts we're trying to reach. Listening to Phil made me realize how hard it's going to be to sell."

Five minutes earlier, I had hated Phil for what he'd said, but in less than a minute Michael had me seeing a part of myself that I hadn't been able to acknowledge before. Every support group meeting raised more and more issues we needed to grapple with in our writing. When would we ever sign off on the article when there was so much to address? Would we ever feel it was done? The number of AIDS cases was climbing past 700, the media wasn't reporting on AIDS and gay men were still resistant to the deadly dangers they were facing. Something had to wake them up. Trying week after week to get our article done was agony.

Then, one night after getting home from an exhausting writing session at Michael's, my doorbell rang.

"Who is it?"

"Tom from Connecticut. Your phone was disconnected. Are you okay?"

"I'm not working anymore, Tom."

"I drove all the way in just to see you. Please, can't I just come up and say hi?"

I buzzed him in not knowing what I would say. Like some of my other clients, he had written letters to me after I disconnected my phones but I didn't want to write back, I wanted to send copies of the article we were writing.

"Look," I told him, "there's something terrible going on with having sex these days and we've got to wake up and stop fucking around until we understand what's happening. Gay men are getting sick and some are dying. I haven't had sex in months."

"You're okay, aren't you?"

"I'm fine," I lied. Tom wanted sex and he wanted it now, and I wanted the $100. But what could we do? I felt frustrated and upset—totally out of character for the S&M top Tom knew, vulnerable and clueless.

"You know, if you think about it, most of what we used to do wasn't actual sex." He fell to his knees, grabbing the back of my legs, and he began to plead. "Please Master, I need you so bad. Can

you take off your sneakers and put on your boots? Just let me worship you and jerk off."

Suddenly it struck me that Tom was right: we could have virtually the same scene we always had with one difference—not putting my dick in his mouth.

I cupped my hands on the back of his head and began pressing
his face against my growing hard-on. What else could we do that
wouldn't spread germs, just using my voice and hands and mind? I
could play with his nipples; he loved that. I could tease him with
my dick without putting it inside him. My mind began racing with
possibilities.

I had a bunch of disposable latex examination gloves I'd taken
from Dr. Sonnabend's office that I used to blow up into huge bal-
loons. (I was picking up a lot of strange habits since I stopped having sex.) I grabbed one and put it on to play with his butt. I didn't
have to do it, but I longed to hear that rapturous moaning that only
seemed to come from the pleasure of penetration.

As soon as Tom began groaning, my face lit up with elation. It
was a moment of epiphany—my erotic baptism into a new age.
Not only did this form of S&M—safe, protective, and caring—feel
fantastic, but I was struck by the realization that I can still be a gay
man and enjoy being sexual without posing risks to my partner or
myself.

As I slid the glove off my hand, I felt just like Dr. Sonnabend in
his office. Although this was in a completely different context, what
was I doing with this client in terms of physical contact that Joe
didn't do examining AIDS patients?

It turned out to be the hottest session Tom and I ever shared.
In addition to the usual rush of adrenaline that I felt running an
S&M scene, the pleasure was further intensified by conquering the
fear of AIDS through having a sexual scene that was freed from the
risks of diseases. After we washed up, I laid down on my platform

bed grinning and motioned Tom to come lie on top of me. As I wrapped my arms tightly around him and held him, he let out a happy, inner-child sigh. "Do you know how long I've been waiting for you to do *this* to me, Master?"

After all the suffering I had seen in the support group, I felt sad that I was still waiting for clients to make the first move when it came to affection. When I began S&M hustling, some clients were turned off if I talked about who I was or about being gay because it got in their way of the Master fantasy. I learned to be a blank page they could fill with whatever erotic details they desired. I erred on the side of caution and money and withheld any post-sex affection unless I could see a sign that they wanted it. But as I held Tom in my arms, I felt I was being transformed. The days of reticence about expressing affection to men I had sex with were over. Maybe that was easier said than done, but Tom had just brought something inside me back to life that I had conditioned myself to repress when I started S&M hustling.

As soon as Tom left, I plopped down at my typewriter, dumbfounded by this startling new experience. Maybe there were lots of ways to have sexual pleasure without taking risks for AIDS. I rolled a piece of paper into my typewriter and typed "How to Have Sex in an Epidemic"; then, realizing that most gay men preferred kissing, sucking, and fucking to fingers/dildoes/manual playing and psychodramas, I humbly added, "One Approach." Seeing those words on the page made me want to dance. I put Grace Jones's "Do or Die" on the stereo and I began bopping around the apartment. This was incredible. This was salvation.

And then I thought of Phil Lanzarratta, and it all came crashing down.

I'd thought AIDS was my wake-up call to be done with this sort of loveless sex, but the minute the opportunity presented itself, I'd jumped right back in, and without feeling any ethical obligation to tell Tom that I was sick. It hadn't even occurred to me to tell him. How would he have reacted if I had? Would he have stayed or freaked out that I might have made him sick from our past scenes? I didn't have full-blown AIDS, but I knew I was immune deficient with swollen glands all over my body and that I could still come down with it. Like Phil, I had just had sex without telling my partner I had an early form of AIDS. I believed what we did posed no harm, but I wouldn't have done it if I had to first tell Tom I was sick. Worst of all, could I be discovering ways to have sex and avoid AIDS after it was too late for me to survive? That would be agony.

And it was the unbearable truth that safe sex came too late for Callen, for my closest friends, and tens of thousands of gay men of my generation. What I was beginning to discover with Tom could have been our salvation, but it would end up breaking our hearts when we realized it had come too late. That painful recognition would eventually lead me to depths of despair and addiction I never could have imagined in the early years of AIDS. Surrounded by a whirlwind of suffering and death, I was too distracted to notice that something had begun eating away at my spirit.

The morning after my scene with Tom, I ran to Dr. Sonnabend's office to tell him and Michael what had happened.

"Isn't that just wonderful," Callen said in a caustic yet humorous tone. "He can whip and beat people without spreading AIDS."

"I have news for you, it was the hottest scene this client and I ever had—and without any hitting," I retorted.

"Well this is something we need to sort out," Dr. Sonnabend said. "It's become quite obvious to anyone with direct experience that it's the anal-receptive partner who is at greatest risk, particularly when one is having multiple sexual partners, whether it's in a bathhouse or a bedroom. If there's one thing we could do to make an impact on the spread of this disease, it would be to point out the danger of receptive anal intercourse without undermining the act itself. One should avoid getting semen inside your partner's rectum, but one must celebrate the act. I've seen it in my practice—guys who don't think twice about having sex when they know they could be giving an infection to their partner, no sense of responsibility or community. If gay men are ever going to curb these diseases there must be a new sense of caring about one's partners. Promiscuity is like a community swimming pool, the more sick people jump in the more polluted the water gets for everyone, including themselves."

"I didn't tell the client last night that I was sick, but nothing we did could have exposed him to anything," I said.

"But you want that to be his choice and you made it for him," Dr. Sonnabend said. "How do I explain that what we were doing posed no risk for AIDS when he hasn't even heard of AIDS?" I asked.

"And now that we're having this discussion, I am even more uncertain how to tell gay men to stop having promiscuous sex," Michael answered. "I don't think we can peddle that message yet, I don't see any way around it. Maybe because I've been so sick and turned off to sex I thought we had to say stop. But I had sex with my lover twice last weekend, and it made me realize, no matter how sick or turned off I get, desire pops back. Look at Richard, I can see him already itching to get back to hustling."

I felt angry and offended by that remark, but I couldn't express that to Michael. I was beginning to develop a crippling survivor's guilt that prevented me from arguing or saying anything negative to gay men who were sick or dying. It hurt me that he couldn't see that I was so eager to do something meaningful with my life, like writing about AIDS. How could I even consider returning to sex work when most gay men still didn't understand a tidal wave of suffering and death was heading our way? Plus, I now felt disgusted at the way some S&M scenes turned suffering into erotic play when all this real suffering was about to consume gay men's lives. I just knew in my bones that I could be useful by writing. Public speaking was Michael's domain.

I told Michael and Dr. Sonnabend, "I keep running into guys I know on the streets who don't want to hear a word about AIDS. They were so terrified, they told me to shut up about it or they would walk away; there's no way they'd be willing to discuss it before having sex."

"But that won't last," Dr. Sonnabend said. "In the meantime, one should try to find ways to approach sex safely while trying to encourage some sort of sexual ethic to promote responsibility. Different men will require different advice, but saying that one should stop sex completely suggests that sexual expression has no value, and that is contradictory to human nature. Sex is a vital part of being alive."

Michael jumped in. "But I don't see how we can effect change at sex clubs like the Mineshaft. As long as there are commercial sex establishments where complete strangers can have multiple partners in silence and darkness while drugged out of their minds, preaching ethics won't clean out that community pool."

"I began typing something last night about different sex scenes that might be safe," I told them, "but most of what I came up with was more about S&M and assplay than regular sex."

"You can find ways to reduce or eliminate the risks for regular sex, like using condoms," Dr. Sonnabend said.

I sat there, dumbfounded. It was the first time I even thought of putting a condom on my dick, in spite of having put a latex glove on my hand.

"Now that I think about it, there are ways to have sex that interrupt disease transmission. That's something you should both write about."

"'Interrupt disease transmission'—what a great way to put it," I said.

"Gay men use condoms? I can't imagine it even though it makes perfect sense," Michael said.

"Putting on a rubber could be seen as an expression of showing one's sexual partner caring, affection, and a desire to protect," Dr. Sonnabend answered. "If that's too difficult to eroticize, gay men really are doomed. Don't you two see that this is the heart of the matter? The people who hate gay men, who want to see them all dead, would be happy if gay men fucked each other to the grave. There's nothing radical about men fucking each other, especially when there's lots of people, like bathhouse owners, doctors, drug companies who can make a fortune from it. The real threat homosexual men pose to America is that if men were able to truly love one another, they might end up giving away for free what this greedy system we live in requires them to sell at the highest possible price."

Michael and I turned to each other stunned by Joe's observation. In one angry breath, the so-called "clap doctor" catapulted our consciousness to a higher plane.

"I saw some Reagan worshipper boasting on television that 'the business of America is business,'" Dr. Sonnabend continued. "He was such a repulsive man, but he's right—and *men loving men is bad for business!* It's downright un-American!"

"Listen to this," I said. "Here's the pamphlet Gay Men's Health Crisis and the gay doctors group, New York Physicians for Human Rights (NYPHR) are distributing in the gay bars. It's really confusing. It says, 'If you think or suspect that you have any diseases that you could give someone else, don't risk the health of others by having sex. Wait until your doctor says it's okay. There is no conclusive evidence that any drug or sexual act causes AIDS, but until we know better you might consider giving up drugs. Current opinion points to something like a virus that may be transmitted sexually, so therefore it makes sense to have as much sex as you want but with fewer partners and with healthy people. If you don't know your partner, ask about his health'—"

"Ask about his health?" Dr. Sonnabend interrupted. "And if someone believes or says it's okay, then what? And what about me, if I've got AIDS? That's what I want to know—what should I do? They've forgotten to address that particular problem. And what about all the guys who are already immune deficient but who don't yet have AIDS? Are they only concerned about advice for the guys who don't have it? If they think they can protect themselves by asking someone in a bathhouse if they're healthy before they have sex, that's giving a false sense of security. That's no protection—that's lethal advice. And they're already implying that if someone is having a lot of different partners, then they probably aren't healthy. Gay men in New York City are the tip of the iceberg of this epidemic. What are they supposed to do? Find partners who don't live a promiscuous lifestyle like themselves? We may be entitled to take chances with our own health, *but what about the other person?*

"They're saying that promiscuity is a game of Russian roulette, but then they don't want to tell gay men to throw the gun away. They buy into this killer-virus theory and then they can't be rational about the ramifications of it, that if you think you're healthy you can go out and take your chances of getting or spreading a killer virus. They don't even understand how damaging what they're saying is—it could be inviting quarantine. You know, when I first heard the CDC talking about the single-virus theory I just couldn't believe how GMHC was going along with it. I wrote letters to Congressmen warning about the potential dangers of saying this; that gay people could be perpetuating such a theory before there is evidence to support it made me think these guys are beyond repair."

"I agree, we have to address the current advice that's out there in our article," Michael said. "We have to show how embracing the killer-virus theory may appear to take the blame off of promiscuity—oops, bad luck, I just happened to catch a killer virus—but it cripples our ability to rationally respond."

"But understand why: their denial about the health hazards of promiscuity playing a causative role in this disease runs so deep that they can talk about catching a sexually transmitted killer virus as a merely a case of bad luck, detached from the behavior that spreads it," Dr. Sonnabend said. "If a gay man goes to the baths and has sex with four people and ends up with syphilis, is that just a case of bad luck? But at the same time, you must not dismiss the single-virus theory out of hand because even though there is no evidence yet to support it, there is also no evidence yet to justify dismissing it. There's actually a long historical debate in science about whether disease is caused by a single agent or the outcome of multifactorial processes which goes back to Hippocrates. The Greeks used to think in a multifactorial sense. They thought that healthy people were the ones who lived in harmony with their surroundings and that when you got sick, it wasn't because a germ or a virus visited you. It was because you didn't eat right, or you got too much heat or were stressed out—things that were a part of you but just not in balance. But those who favor a single virus or specific etiology say none of that matters—all that matters is you caught a germ. Generally speaking, there are no viruses, even rabies, which make everybody who is infected sick. There are people exposed who don't get sick, so there are obviously other factors, and those factors may include your overall health, which when it's good, makes you much less likely to get sick when you come into contact with germs. Saying that AIDS is merely the result of some mysterious virus in a population of gay men who have been exposed to so many sexually transmitted diseases and other factors, is shortsighted. It puts blinders on your thinking when what's needed is to keep probing, asking questions, leaving all avenues of research open for investigation.

"When something new comes along, scientists will create new theories to try and figure out what's going on. But one can account for things that are new by recombining old influences in new ways. It's more complicated than just a germ. It means one must do a little thinking. What I have proposed isn't meant as the definitive answer but rather a conceptual framework for looking at this disease to suggest avenues of research. I think a brief paragraph that says you guys want to do a follow-up that's more hopeful is all that is needed here."

"I think we're right to argue that the party is over," Michael said. "The party was about sexual abandon—acting on any and every sexual desire that came our way and doing whatever drug was put in front of us. That has to stop. There were some good things about the '70s—but the pigging-out-on-sex subculture that led us to view our bodies as mere playthings has to change, and that's the target audience for our article. We do believe the explosion of commercial sex establishments helped set the stage for the explosion of AIDS, and if we are to explain Joe's theory we can't be squeamish about pointing that out. Face it, you two: a generation of gay men who celebrated a decade of complete sexual abandon with hundreds of partners is not going to settle down into monogamy or using condoms overnight. Our first article has to focus on waking gay men up to this catastrophe and explain what we believe is causing it. Then we can work on a second piece on how to respond constructively to this crisis.

"Maybe Michael is right," Joe said. "It has become a lethal way of life. Perhaps American men are conditioned just to see each other as competitors and customers; perhaps they don't have the empathy or the willingness to sacrifice some personal pleasure in order to protect one other. It's terribly sad, but if gay men can't see their interconnectedness spiritually, they may have to be woken up to it microbiologically."

By the beginning of November, Michael had taken our article, "We Know Who We Are," to the office of the *New York Native*. Not only did the *Native* publisher, Charles Ortleb, agree to publish our piece—the editor, Brett Averill, changed only a few words in three entire newspaper pages of print. It was the longest article they had ever published. Ortleb told Michael that he was showing our article to some gay leaders and that he was running a rebuttal to our arguments in the same issue. Obviously, we had struck a nerve or scared the hell out of them, and we were worried about what the rebuttal would say.

At the eleventh hour, as "We Know Who We Are" was going to press, Michael called me in a panic to tell me that Ortleb had subtitled our article, "Two Gay Men Declare War on Promiscuity."

"No! We can't let them! It sets us up to be hated."

"I know it does. I pleaded with them to drop it. They're putting it in a box on the cover."

"They're using us to sell papers—it's tabloid mentality."

"Brett is a sweetheart, but Ortleb got on the phone and he was so mean to me. He yelled, 'It runs with that subtitle or not at all,' and slammed the phone down. I felt like I'd been slugged."

"Maybe he's bluffing. He can't pull it now—it's coming out to-morrow."

"Oh, yes, he can. He also knows we can't just take it to another gay publication—there is no other gay publication. Let's look at this from his point of view. Most of his advertisers are sex-related businesses. He is going out on a limb publishing us, though I think on some level, he favors our message."

"So sacrifice the messengers."

"Let's decide this together. What do you want us to do?"

"I'm bursting to get this out already. He's got us over a barrel."

"I'm afraid he does."

"Why can't he subtitle it, 'Two Gay Men Declare War on Sexually Transmitted Diseases'?"

"It's not open to discussion, and you better face it, Richard, even though I feel that subtitle encourages gay men to hate our article before they read a word of it, we *are* saying the party's over."

I knew that, but there was something about the scene with my client Tom, and the growing heap of cards and letters from former clients desperately trying to track me down, that kept nagging me with doubts that it was all over. Michael didn't buy my argument that what Tom and I did was safe, hot, and caring, but since he was the one facing death from AIDS each day, and I had grown to love him, I bowed to his conviction and I thanked God I wasn't in his shoes.

"Prepare to be hated," Michael continued. "But look, it's a miracle in newspaper publishing to run such a long piece and they hardly changed a word of what we submitted. That's almost unheard of for neophytes like us. Let's focus on that and remember this article will surely spark debate and we'll have the chance to address this and many other issues when that happens."

After three months, it was done. The *Native* was featured prominently on every newsstand in the city, right next to the *New York Times* and *Daily News*. At long last, instead of sounding like a lunatic every time I tried to explain Sonnabend's complicated theory about AIDS to someone I bumped into on the street, I could just hand them a copy of our article. I felt such profound relief.

But it wouldn't last long.

5

Confessions of a Condom-Maniac

The author, 1983

In the first week of November 1982, our article hit the newsstands of Manhattan. "We Know Who We Are: Two Gay Men Declare War on Promiscuity" was about to ignite a firestorm of debate that at least helped awaken a community still unaware of the magnitude of the threat posed by AIDS. Here is a condensed version:

> Those of us who have lived a life of excessive promiscuity on the urban gay circuit of bathhouses, backrooms, balconies, sex clubs, meat racks and tearooms know

who we are. We could continue to deny overwhelming evidence that the present health crisis is a direct result of the unprecedented promiscuity that has occurred since Stonewall, but such denial is killing us. Denial will continue to kill us until we begin the difficult task of changing the ways in which we have sex.

What do we mean by "excessive promiscuity"? Though it has not been reported in the national or gay press, the National Cancer Institute . . . stated in March 1982: "The median number of lifetime male sexual partners for homosexual patients with AIDS is 1,160."

Few have been willing to say it so clearly, but the single greatest risk factor for contracting AIDS is a history of multiple sexual contacts with partners who are having multiple sexual contacts—that is, sex on the circuit. We know who we are. . . .

We believe that it is the *accumulation of risk* through leading a promiscuous gay urban lifestyle, which has led to the breakdown of immune responses that we are seeing now. Most published medical reports indicate that continued re-exposure and re-infection with common viruses . . . in conjunction with other common venereal infections and perhaps other factors, have led to the present health crisis among urban gay promiscuous men. . . .

One cannot presume that this is the first epidemic of AIDS in history. Since the ability of medical science to detect indicators of immunosuppression is [two years old], one must ask: (1) how long have there been individuals with collapsed immune systems; and (2) how long have such individuals been recognized and observed in classic epidemiologic terms?

It is possible that immunosuppression has existed for as long as there have been viruses; admittedly, there is no way to verify this hypothesis. However, review of autopsy reports in the U.S. going back 30 years has indicated the possibility that AIDS may have existed in a limited fashion as early as 1950 (Williams et al., *The Lancet,* 1960, 2:951–955; P. Nichols, *The New England Journal of Medicine,* April 15, 1982, pp. 934–935). Similar autopsy review in Denmark indicates the possibility of AIDS at least since 1963 (Jensen et al., *The Lancet,* May 1, 1982; cf. Clemensen letter, *The Lancet,* July 3, 1982).

Empirical verification of these reports as evidence of AIDS is impossible since the tests which detect immune deficiency have only recently come into use. . . .

People are dying—very real, horrible and unnecessary deaths. Sure the baths are fun; but the risks have simply become too great. A year ago, new cases were being reported at the rate of one a day; today, the rate is three times that. . . .

Rely on no single source for your information: not your doctor, not this newspaper, not the Gay Men's Health Crisis, not the CDC. Educate yourself now so that if and when the time comes, you can make informed medical decisions about treatment—and your life. . . .

Disease has changed the definition of promiscuity. What ten years ago was viewed as a healthy reaction to a sex-negative culture now threatens to destroy the very fabric of urban gay male life. . . .

The 13 years since Stonewall have demonstrated tremendous change. So must the next 13 years.

As 1982 was coming to an end, most Americans had no way of knowing what the occasional news reports on AIDS might portend, but a seismic shift in sexual behavior wasn't waiting for public awareness—it was already underway. Annual surveillance reports compiled by city health departments in charge of tracking cases of sexually transmitted infections revealed a new kind of precedent: After more than a decade of ever-increasing STI rates among gay men in cities where AIDS had struck hard and early, led by New York City and San Francisco, the numbers were suddenly *dropping*. Back in our support group, where meetings were packed to capacity and competition for time to speak was fierce, these statistics came to life in tales men told. Some of the most sexually active gay men were being abruptly rendered celibate by a long, grisly list of opportunistic infections that comprised the deadly new syndrome. With increasing frequency, chilling tales about what was happening spread quickly through each man's inner circle, then carried fear and panic through the urban gay grapevine, sparking periodic pauses and even permanent farewells to that beloved pastime, cruising for sex. The confusing AIDS risk reduction brochures put out by the New York Physicians for Human Rights that were appearing in gay bars succeeded in raising awareness but sent anxiety levels soaring. In the bars, at the gym, or on a Sunday stroll down Christopher Street, a palpable sense of alarm seemed to hang in the air, a foreboding that something awful was unfolding, something so momentous it strained comprehension and credulity until one of those circulating stories turned out to be someone you knew. Those haunting pangs of worry and fear were like an annoying visitor that didn't know when to leave and was difficult to get rid of, until somewhere between the hospital visits and the funeral service, it moved in to stay.

That sorrowful awakening touched the lives of many New Yorkers, but for gay men it changed everything, dividing life as we knew it in two: before AIDS and after AIDS. For me, that perception lasted three days following my biopsy. As soon as Joe Sonnabend said I could survive, I became an instant believer. People believe what they want to believe or allow themselves to be led to believe, and survival seemed as valid as anything else to believe. I put my faith in hope, but I had a scientific theory to back it up. There was one thing, however, I didn't have: the slightest expectation that there would be a price to pay—and that was my sense of belonging to the gay community.

Those first declines in the soaring rates of STIs among urban gay men marked a sea change in the celebration of sexual freedom noted, among other places, in the acclaimed 1977 book *The Joy of Gay Sex*. "Male homosexuality as it is today is a brand new phenomenon," the book's first sentence declared. "[M]odern gay life has no antecedents. The gay lifestyle that has evolved in the last hundred years and acquired many of its distinctive features only in the last two decades would have made no sense at all to the homosexuals of the past."

That's what Dr. Sonnabend believed as he considered what factors could be playing a role in the development of AIDS and in trying to answer the question, "Why is the epidemic of AIDS happening now?" But as gay activists started waking up to a catastrophe of unimaginable proportions, acute concern about the potential ramifications of every question asked and every answer given was filtered through a collective fear of what our many enemies and too few allies might think and do. After an explosive community meeting Callen attended, he called me to report a statement made by a gay physician who would soon be appointed a citywide leader in the fight against AIDS: "I'm not concerned with reality—I'm concerned with appearances." That upside down placement of priorities was about to become a formidable obstacle to the one hope that could save some of our imperiled lives, the distinctly urban, anal-centric, gay male invention of safe sex. A battle was looming. After months of the horror and misery that Callen and I were witnessing in our support group meetings and in light of Dr. Sonnabend's despair over the lack of a reporter he considered "adequate to the task of documenting the full enormity of this tragedy," there was little chance that we would water down our safe sex manifesto to make it more presentable for the general public in the Reagan era—to whitewash a theory we believed could explain AIDS and save lives. The risk through vaginal intercourse had not yet been established. The booklet we were now planning, *How to Have Sex in an Epidemic: One Approach,* targeted sexually active gay men.

When the onslaught of AIDS first became apparent, brief but colorful debates erupted about our varied sexual lifestyles, but they were soon contained for the sake of gay unity. Most gay men were waking up to the age of AIDS frightened, bewildered, and uncertain about what to believe and whom to trust. Despite the occasional positive portrayals of lesbians and gay men in TV movies, gays barely existed in the national media, and when we did, outright contempt, usually in the form of Jerry Falwell, continued to be a standard component to "balancing" any gay-related news story. Gay leaders and activists were terrified that the media's coverage of AIDS was going to increase discrimination and anti-gay violence and lead to quarantining thousands of us and even to some form of concentration camps. The first two fears proved true for gay Americans; the second fear was reserved for new immigrants. The last fear may seem hysterical today, but it was seen as a genuine possibility among some early AIDS activists whose concerns, twenty years later, are easier to understand in the context of the climate of that time when a terrifying plague began to unfold and so little was known. But informing gay men about the mortal threat of AIDS remained the responsibility of the national media at a bad time, an ascendancy of right-wing thinking ushered in by President Reagan. In that chilling social and political climate, early AIDS activists began to confront the tortuous prospect of balancing the potential political consequences of what they said in public about the most private aspects of human behavior with health concerns that were now an urgent matter of life and death. Hanging in the balance was safe sex, the one hope each of us at risk held in our own hands, if we could just figure out in time what exactly safe sex was.

⇐   ⇒

"I'm waking you again," Callen lamented over the phone.

"I was up late writing the safe sex article but I really need your help."

"I'm still recuperating from our last tome. You write it and I'll help with editing."

"I can't do this without you. I'll just keep bugging you until you make time."

"Richard, I have an anal yeast infection, a herpes outbreak, an active case of mono, and a full-time paralegal job, so forgive me if I'm not in the mood right now."

"Let me read you something I wrote but try to refrain from laughing at me like last time," I said.

"It was the way you fired off that interminable list of S&M activities, added a comma, and said, these are just a *few* of the things you can do safely. A *few!* I could have baked a batch of cookies while you were reading that roster."

I read: "'Some sexually active gay men may find these guidelines for medically safe sex severe or unmanageable. If you do, my advice is, clip and save.'"

"You do have a certain S&M style."

"Damn, what if I add, 'because I felt that way a short time ago'?"

"Now you nailed it," said Michael. "But realize gay men reading this will be predisposed to hate you no matter how you say it: Once again someone is presuming to tell them how they should have sex, which ipso facto is an arrogant thing to do. Some will say, if sex has to be this mechanical, looking at everyone as if they might kill me, it's not worth it."

"Then they'll be identifying themselves as the future victims of AIDS."

"But what if AIDS is primarily a bottom's disease, as Joe has suspected? Six months in our support group is convincing me tops don't get AIDS."

"What makes you so sure?" I asked.

"Just that I've shamelessly interrogated absolutely everybody in our group and the only one who doesn't call himself a bottom is you, my dear."

"Most of the sex I've had has been as a top. But whenever I've done certain drugs, the desire to get fucked kicks in. Call me a repressed bottom, because I don't feel the urge sober; it's always been tied to drugs. But when I discovered Ecstasy while hustling, I was really getting into it at the baths and relaxing my concern about getting STIs. That's when Joe started confronting me and trying to yank me out of it when I started showing up with anal gonorrhea."

"So according to Joe's theory," Michael surmised, "you accumulated enough assaults on your immune system to make you immune deficient, but not to the level where your blood test results put you in the range where AIDS patients get opportunistic infections."

"None of my abnormal counts are far from the normal range, but they are precisely the ones that define AIDS. Even though Joe believes my biopsy was necessary to rule out Hodgkin's disease,

I'm convinced it was a desperate attempt to wake me up. That's why I'm proud of 'We Know Who We Are.' It's my chance to try and give gay men the wake-up call Joe gave me."

"I'm relieved to hear you say that," said Michael, "because I've been sensing ambivalence in you. Even if we overstated some things, we'll never regret trying to alert gay men when there's 10,000 cases, but I feel like you're rushing to get the safe sex article out to head off the inevitable attacks on what we wrote instead of preparing to confront them."

"My friends said that reading 'We Know Who We Are' scared the hell out of them. Our goal was to wake them up, and we did. Let's move on because when I explained what I'm writing now with Joe, they said, fuck theories, just tell us how to protect ourselves when we have sex."

"But it has to be based on some rationale. You can't just tell gay men what to do."

"That is a major career adjustment," I answered, "which is why I'm pleading for your help."

"Keep reading René Dubos's *Man Adapting*. It's the bible of the multifactorial view of disease. I realized Joe isn't just saying AIDS is multifactorial, but *all* diseases are multifactorial. That's the only theoretical basis now for proposing medically safe sex."

"Dubos is depressing. He says the debate over whether diseases are the outcome of a single germ or a constellation of factors has been raging for 2,000 years. We're on the losers' side of a controversy that dates back to Jesus."

"Get your copy of *For Her Own Good* [by Barbara Ehrenreich and Deirdre English] and look up Germ Theory in the index."

I did and began reading: "'Traditional religion saw individual disease as the price of moral failings, epidemics as acts of a vengeful God. But, through the lenses of the new high-power microscopes available in the mid-1800s, disease began to look like a natural event which depended less on God than on the growth rates of what appeared to be fairly amoral species of microbes. . . . Germ Theory did not forge quite as firm a link between medicine and bacteriology as the scientific doctors liked to think. It is true that by 1900 specific germs had been associated with typhoid, leprosy, tuberculosis, cholera, diphtheria and tetanus—but in what sense the germs *caused* the diseases was not so clear.'"

"That's what Dr. Sonnabend is suggesting about AIDS," said Michael. "Here is his best analogy yet for AIDS. If a person has a heart attack, they don't think, this must have happened because of that pat of butter I put on my toast last Tuesday. Heart disease is understood as a multifactorial process because well-funded research has led to our understanding that many factors can contribute to heart disease. No one has a problem accepting that poor diet, stress, lack of exercise, smoking, genetics, increasing age, and other factors can lead to a heart attack, and no one gets accused of blaming the victim for saying these things. Why are gay men whose lives are most at risk so defensive about leaving the door open to consider more than one causative factor leading to a disease syndrome as complicated as AIDS? Are we going to put political concerns over life-and-death medical concerns? *For Her Own Good* makes the prescient point that sometimes in a crisis, the greatest damage is done by people who believe that they have your best interests at heart because whether it's medical paternalism or political paternalism, good intentions can become blinders."

"That's scary but brilliant," I said. "Every free moment Joe has between patients and phone calls I'm picking his brain about sex acts. What's the risk if you suck but don't let someone come in your mouth? Where's the risk in getting sucked? I ended up following him into the bathroom barking questions with my notepad until he gave me a look of death. I can be relentless, but I get the sense that he thinks my focus on sex acts misses his main point that there has to be affection between sexual partners to ensure mutual responsibility. He said we don't need to create a new sexual ethic but rediscover an old sensibility of caring about each other so that you don't end up as some anonymous object, as just a body. But what if certain forms of sexual expression that we don't see as particularly affirming or positive can be made safer? Aren't we obliged to advise ways to reduce or eliminate risk or are we endorsing those activities if we do? I can't stop thinking about some of my regulars who could benefit from advice but whose particular sexual tastes all three of us have mocked among ourselves. When gay men wake up to what's going on in our support group, nothing will remain the same, they'll see what we've learned, that—"

"—we are our brother's keeper," Michael finished the thought. "Then you need to find the common ground between what you just told me and what Joe keeps emphasizing."

In the months after the publication of "We Know Who We Are," a storm of controversy erupted as angry reactions appeared in the *Native* and other publications. Dr. Sonnabend urged us not to be sidetracked by personal attacks or by published misrepresentations of what we had written. But engaging our community in debate was a goal Callen and I had in writing it; once the guys in our support group told us that what we'd written made sense, we were eager to go forward.

But what we didn't realize was that most gay men got their information from mainstream media, which didn't wake up to the magnitude and gravity of AIDS until the following spring of 1983. Just a half dozen stories totaling about fifteen minutes appeared in all of 1982 on ABC, CBS, and NBC nightly news broadcasts. As a result, during the first two crucial years, most sexually active gay men at risk for AIDS were only peripherally aware of it and had little reason to believe it was going to directly affect them. But for those of us already fighting full time on the frontlines in 1982, we knew it was just a matter of time until AIDS became an acute national concern.

In the meantime, an astonishing lack of concern was evident even in the gay press. The leftist Toronto-based *Body Politic: A Magazine for Gay Liberation* published two feature stories on AIDS that hit the newsstands on the same day that "We Know Who We Are" appeared, but their position was diametrically opposed to ours. Worst of all, how could safe sex be understood or embraced by people stuck on minimizing AIDS as a minor heath problem maximizing it as a political affront. In "Living with Kaposi's," Michael Lynch argued that gay men were becoming unnecessarily panicked over AIDS due to "a persistent, anti-sexual sense of guilt" that if left unchecked could "rip apart the very promiscuous fabric that knits the gay male community together." In a companion article, "The Real Gay Epidemic: Panic and Paranoia," Dr. Bill Lewis wrote, "In the same period that 200 AIDS cases were diagnosed, more than 400 gay men died in traffic accidents because they chose to go outside." He warned, "Lesbians and sexually active gay men are going to have their rights denied and infringed upon—all because 400 cases of a disease have appeared among 20 million of us."

Callen was quick to fire off a response. "If one gay person were killed in any gay demonstration, the pages of *Body Politic* would scream with outrage and a call to revolution. But when hundreds of gay men die from a sexually transmitted disease, the guardians of gay liberation cluck about 'over-reaction.' What kind of doctor is it who puts political considerations over the tragedy of even one gay man's death? It astounds me that I have to point out that all this 'panic' is because *gay men are dying!* By refusing to see that the promiscuous lifestyle is potentially fatal, we may permit the ultimate triumph of the Moral Majority: *we will kill ourselves.*"

That marked the first public skirmish in a contentious debate about the cause of AIDS that would determine the future of safe sex. It was fall 1982. HIV had not yet been identified. There were many theories about the cause of AIDS, but two main ones emerged. One theory, the single-virus theory, argued that a new sexually transmitted virus was the cause of AIDS. The other theory, the multifactorial theory, argued that AIDS was the result from an accumulated immunosuppressive burden resulting from multiple sexually transmitted infections (STIs) that were so prevalent among those gay men who were developing AIDS at that time. This theory was supported by research published in 1981 through 1982 in the leading scientific journals that Dr. Sonnabend had given me to read the day he told me I wasn't about to die of AIDS. Dr. Sonnabend proposed his own theoretical model of how many different factors might interact to produce AIDS. It was published in several scientific journals and books, but the first time it appeared in publication was in the *Journal of the American Medical Association* in May 1983 (vol. 249, no. 17, pp. 2370–2374.)

These two different views have many different implications. A single virus as the cause of AIDS makes it easy to downplay behavioral factors, such as promiscuity and drug use. It offers the hope of a chemical cure with little or no need to change behavior or to look at the impact on health of how people live or of social conditions such as poverty. It implied that a single exposure could cause AIDS. It appeals to the high-tech obsession of our society and our faith in science to come up with a cure. It places little importance on the effects of lifestyle on health: when something goes wrong, science will provide a remedy.

The multifactorial view, on the other hand, puts a great deal of importance on behavior and social conditions. And, significantly to the development of safe sex at that time, it considered a single exposure unlikely to produce the syndrome of diseases that made up AIDS.

The dichotomy between these two theories created tremendous tensions. The religious right liked the single-virus theory. It saw the sexual revolution as an affront to the right's religious values. If a killer virus was being randomly transmitted through a single sexual contact it gave them a powerful argument against infidelity: one act of adultery could kill. But it was bizarre to see who else liked this theory: gay men. The single-virus theory offered a way to look at AIDS and absolve promiscuity as having any contributory role to the development of this disease. As one gay spokesperson stated emphatically in the media, "AIDS is a virus; it could have landed among housewives in Des Moines. It just happened to land in the gay community."

In the 1970s, some gay writers and activists promoted promiscuity as representing the height of gay male liberation. Sexual gay liberation saw itself as the radical antithesis to the heterosexual monogamous model. Some of these gay men assumed a defensive leadership role when AIDS emerged only a decade later. We can only imagine how difficult it must have been for them to accept that their encouragement of sexual promiscuity in the 1970s may have unknowingly contributed to the deaths of tens of thousands of gay men. And so, for very different reasons, it seemed that gay men joined hands with those who despised them—the religious right—to rapidly endorse the single-virus theory.

In the early years, some gay leaders continued to defend promiscuity despite the exploding epidemic, conveniently forgetting that even if they were right, it was still behavior that spread the killer virus. On the other hand, the multifactorial theory gave a central role to promiscuity and focused on this, provoking the hostility of the gay leadership. What could be more painful than confronting the possibility that one may have contributed to thousands of deaths of their own people by unwittingly celebrating or promoting promiscuity, as some had?

The first criticism of "We Know Who We Are" was an attack on the multifactorial theory that was making the invention of safe sex possible. In the December 6, 1982, issue of the *Native*, Charles Jurrist's "In Defense of Promiscuity: Hard Questions about Real Life" stated that Callen and I were among several voices "unleashing . . . hysteria within our community." He cited our "immune overload theory" as being the "most plausible" explanation for why gay men were dying, but then he ignored the bulk of the iceberg underneath the surface. Echoing Dr. Lewis, Jurrist argued that with 716 AIDS cases reported, a gay "man is more likely to be injured or killed in his car . . . than he is to develop AIDS." Demonstrating his own confusion, after stating he favored our theory that the health hazards of promiscuity were crucial to causing AIDS, he nevertheless concluded, "I will continue to be promiscuous. I won't be scared out of seeking fulfillment. Nor will I consider my behavior in any way as self-destructive. I see it as life affirming. I refuse to blight my life in order—supposedly—to preserve it." If a journalist who graduated from Yale was that confused, one can imagine how overwhelmed the average gay man must have been.

It wasn't just the complexity of a new and deadly syndrome of diseases that was staggering to comprehend, or trying to absorb the likelihood that whatever was causing AIDS, the lifestyle you lived and loved put you at risk for it no matter how hard you tried to minimize it. More than anything was the feeling of terror at being swept up into a violent storm like an inconsequential fleck of dust, the way any force of nature, be it a hurricane, earthquake, or plague, can, in a moment, wipe your existence away.

One night while shaving, I noticed two dark spots on my chest. I ran to the phone, called Dr. Sonnabend, told him I thought I might have found Kaposi's sarcoma lesions and was coming right over. I took him into his bathroom, turned on the lights to show him, only to realize the spots were gone. "They were there five minutes ago, I swear." Sonnabend calmed me down, deflected my apology as unnecessary and said we had to make time to do my blood counts the next day. Maybe the results would yield good news. When I got home, I discovered two oval splatters of shaving cream on the mirror of my medicine cabinet that cast shadows on my reflection. I felt ridiculous, relieved yet certain that this wouldn't be the last alarm.

I joined two scientific studies monitoring gay men at risk for AIDS, both of which required taking blood tests, urine samples, and sperm specimens regularly to monitor the immune system. I began keeping a record of all my results, which were becoming a joy to behold; many of my blood counts were improving, some even moving into the normal range for the first time since my bout with hepatitis in 1981. I was determined to become living proof of Sonnabend's contention that, up to a certain point, immune deficiency isn't an inevitable plunge toward death that, amid the growing panic, almost everyone assumed it was.

The *Village Voice* finally made AIDS a cover story in its December 21, 1982, issue. The moment I saw the boldfaced title, "Defenseless," spread across the front page like a banner, I got livid. The most important lesson Dr. Sonnabend instilled in Callen and me was the notion of self-empowerment. "Defenseless" played into the initial hopelessness that I had encountered at my first AIDS support group meeting and captured the mindset of many gay men who long before AIDS had embraced an ideology of victimhood. This was perfectly captured by Dr. Peter Seitzman, president of the New York Physicians for Human Rights, who wrote, "Aunt Tillie did no more to bring on her breast cancer than to be a woman. She is seen as a victim, pure and simple." It was quite a seductive analogy. Simplistic and stupid, but accessible.

For over a decade, the *Village Voice* was unparalleled as an above-ground newspaper that reported regularly and in depth on gay issues, but concerns were mounting about the length of time it was taking to cover a tragedy unfolding in its own backyard. "Defenseless" was Stephen Harvey's personal account of having a pre-AIDS condition. His writing was witty, fanciful, and contained groundless assertions he criticized in other AIDS reporting. He acknowledged that many AIDS patients had been highly promiscuous, but diffused significance in that by stating other AIDS patients hadn't been, or as he put it, "were well-nigh sexual anorectics." How did he know there were gay men with AIDS who didn't have a considerable history of promiscuity? A few AIDS patients he asked said so and Harvey's own doctor agreed.

That contradicted most if not all of the leading scientific journals, which cited multiple health hazards associated with urban gay male promiscuity and developing AIDS. Harvey acknowledged that body of evidence but only to say he "couldn't understand most of it." With the findings of scientific research tossed aside, Harvey undermined that body of data with precision. Personal testimony denying or minimizing one's sexual behavior became facts when published in a newspaper known for its history of investigative journalism that suddenly didn't extend beyond interviewing one's own doctor. Once cases of "sexual anorectics" with AIDS get reported as facts, it moves attempts to connect promiscuity with developing AIDS into another realm, away from science and closer to the legal and religious forces that had persecuted sexual freedom outside marriage for over a century. What kind of person would accuse someone who was suffering with a fatal disease of being a liar and a slut?

One fool stepped up to the plate. I feared the consequences, but at least I'd be around to face them. Most gay men were still in the dark or in denial about AIDS and my blood counts were already getting better. I felt more gratitude than I knew what to do with and I was willing to do almost anything that needed to be done. If gay men failed to see the connection between certain health hazards of promiscuity and developing AIDS, what reason would there be for adopting the restrictions of safe sex?

The day Harvey's article hit the stands, I was at the *Voice* office with two angry letters to the editor, one mine, one Callen's. We didn't expect them to be published, we just hoped to wake up some editors there, but a few hours later, I received a call asking me to return and help shorten my letter for publication. As I headed back, each block felt like walking the plank, on my way to become a Benedict Arnold in the gay community.

The editor was an amiable straight guy who confided to me that what I'd written had caused an uproar in the office. Noting my lack of surprise, he added that it was being published over the fierce objections of gay men on the staff only because the editor-in-chief, David Schneiderman, insisted. I felt numb at the prospect of being given a chance to be heard by straights while the "gay men on the staff," writers I idolized, wanted me silenced. I realized people who were anti-gay could use what I was saying as ammunition, but I couldn't see any other way to save us in the face of a deadly epidemic that was just beginning. This was an existential American crisis: there was no way to bullshit a way around AIDS! I was suddenly struck with the sobering realization that if there was a lie that could protect gay men from AIDS, I could see myself marching down Fifth Avenue with it plastered across a banner: that's who I was and I was no hero.

My letter read like a wake-up call from hell:

> We are not all "defenseless." *The Voice* would have us believe we are; society has conditioned us to feel we are; and as gay men, many of us have come to eroticize defenselessness. But we are not. A growing number of gay men have demonstrated through regular blood tests a steady recovery from our immune suppression since we

stopped being promiscuous and therefore stopped exposing ourselves to viruses and infections that urban gay male promiscuity makes inevitable. I have learned from meeting fellow AIDS victims that over the years we have become numb to [sexually transmitted] disease[s]. We have even learned to joke about it. Harvey has too: "You have the Movie Disease. You have one hour and 49 minutes to live, and you get to wear gray lipstick in the last reel." My friends are watching young gay men die. We don't get the joke.

Harvey replied by attacking me for being arrogant but sounded exposed when he had to admit, "[I]t is apparently true that a small number of 'sexual anorectics' are afflicted with AID[S]; my statement was based on a number of case histories reported to me by the lymphadenopathy specialist who has treated me."

The week my letter appeared in *The Village Voice,* I got a phone call from a CNN producer asking me to appear on a live, forty-minute panel discussion about AIDS. It was a chance to bring Dr. Sonnabend's ideas to a nationwide audience and I did it. The following Monday, the producer asked if it was okay to give out my phone number because they had received many interested calls. I figured I was better than I thought, but it wasn't journalists trying to track me down, it was old clients wanting to come back. I couldn't believe it; they were using CNN as an escort agency.

In the January 3–16, 1983, issue of the *Native,* the attacks against "We Know Who We Are" gained momentum. In "Guilt and AIDS," Dr. Peter Seitzman, president of the New York Physicians for Human Rights, wrote, "But what of those . . . whose guilt is shouted from the rooftops? For it is two of them who stimulated me to write about guilt in the first place . . . Richard Berkowitz and Michael Callen. . . . [T]he real message they impart is their feeling of guilt. It's all our fault, they seem to say . . . it's just us guys being promiscuous, doing all this damage to ourselves. 'The pool of promiscuous partners is . . . highly polluted.' These are not complimentary terms to be using about oneself."

In the following *Native* issue, "The Case Against Medical Panic," by Lawrence Mass, M.D., the world's first AIDS reporter, linked Callen and me with Jerry Falwell and his Moral Majority, classifying us as "right- wingers". Referring to us as "not unlike religious converts," Mass implied that we were "sex-negative propagandists" out to exploit the AIDS epidemic. He accused us of "vigilante impulsivity" and "blaming-the-victim."

GMHC co-founder Nathan Fain stated, in the February 17, 1983 issue of the *Advocate,* that, "Berkowitz and Callen went after 'those of us who have lived a life of excessive promiscuity' and urged them to follow along in self-flagellation. . . . [B]y advertising their guilt so candidly, these men detonated the issue of promiscuity as dangerously as they knew how."

Over the course of the next few weeks, Michael labored intensely on a speech he had been invited to give on the first gay cable TV show, *Our Time,* in Manhattan in February 1983. For weeks he kept reading me new versions by phone, but they all sounded good to me. Here is the final version.

> I am a 27 year old gay man with AIDS and I have been asked to talk about the volatile issue of promiscuity.
>
> "Promiscuity" is a vague word that means different things to different people. But until we develop a better vocabulary, "promiscuity" remains the best word available to describe the historically unique phenomenon of large numbers of urban gay men having large numbers of different sexual partners in such commercialized set-

tings as bathhouses, backrooms, bookstores, balconies and tearooms.

The debate about the role of promiscuity in defining urban gay maleness has been changed utterly and forever because now gay men are dying. Gay men like you and me. To those who understand the reality of AIDS, to those who wake up every morning and examine their bodies for KS lesions, to those who have seen friends and lovers and former tricks waste away like victims of Auschwitz, disfigured by disease—urban gay male promiscuity as we know it today has no defense. The political issues raised by promiscuity are important, but what civil rights do dead men have?

In 1983, walking into the baths and backrooms with the delusion that you can check your responsibility at the door with your clothes, is an act of personal and cultural suicide. Either you do not love life or you do not know death.

What is over isn't sex—just sex without responsibility.

Ending this health emergency begins with each one of us talking responsibility for his own health, and by so doing, insuring the health of his partners. As long as we continue to selfishly ask, "Is that man a health risk to me," without first asking, "Am I a health risk to him," we will never be free from the tyranny of AIDS.

Our challenge is to figure out how to have gay, life-affirming sex, satisfy our emotional needs, and stay alive. Hard questions for hard times, but whatever happened to our great gay imagination?

But even as I listened to a dozen versions of that speech over the phone, it never occurred to me to tell Callen I knew what was happening to some our gay imaginations. Over the months, my doorbell started ringing at all hours of the night while neighbors were sleeping and the only way to stop it was to answer it. I'd drag myself out of bed, usually after four A.M. when the bars in my neighborhood closed. Old pals and clients were worried or wondering why I had disappeared. I gave them of copies of "We Knew Who We Are," I explained what I thought was going on, but where there was a hungry bottom, there was a way. Slowly but surely, my apartment was starting to look like an extension of Dr. Sonnabend's office in the same way that it started looking like a sex shop when I first started hustling and clients kept leaving accoutrements behind. Only now it was boxes of disposable gloves, pharmaceutical company samples of germicidal soaps, etc. I didn't think of it as returning to hustling—I had no ad, no new clients and I was not in the mood for any S&M after being around dying men all day. Plus, my name was being trashed in the gay press with Callen's as the Carrie Nations of promiscuity, hardly a hooker reference. Most gay men were still in denial about AIDS, just like the bar flies, clients, and other escorts that kept showing up at my door at ungodly hours. And I didn't realize at the time that I was in denial too—about retiring from sex work. I kept assuming once we talked about AIDS they wouldn't be in the mood, but Sonnabend was right, we couldn't run away from it and as Callen said, desire has a way of popping back. Some of my best lines in *How to Have Sex in an Epidemic: One Approach* came from those late-night wake-up calls. So it was research, work in the field and it was a bizarre adaptation, but the journey from Beatle bangs, to Polly Political, to gay husband to Vinnie had somehow led a gay man to using his first condoms. It was weird, at first; all I could think about was pregnancy and straight men. But this was the future and I was determined to make condoms an integral part of sex.

In May 1983, the national news media woke up to the enormity of the epidemic and ignited the first outbreak of panic over contagion, which swept the nation. "The toll of illness and death from AIDS continues its relentless climb: 1,366 Americans have now been infected, and 520 of them have died. Amid angry accusations that the federal government has ignored the medical emergency because heterosexuals have largely been spared, the homosexual community rallied last week to take AIDS out of the closet: thousands of victims and sympathizers—both gay and straight—held candlelight vigils across the country and demanded increased public research funds," Jean Seligmann of *Newsweek* reported in their May 16, 1983, issue (p. 94). The article was less than a page, but it ended with a bombshell that would awaken the nation to AIDS in a way that would never be the same again. "'If non-sexual, nonblood-borne transmission is possible,' warns Dr. Anthony Fauci of the National Institutes of Health, 'the scope of the syndrome may be enormous.'"

Fauci had publicly speculated that the cases of AIDS in infants in Newark, New Jersey, might have been transmitted from routine, household contact. Fauci had just tossed a bombshell, which he later retracted under pressure. The multifactorial view would have noted that Newark had widespread poverty. It also had some of the highest rates of unemployment, infant mortality, and IV drug use, and, ever since Reagan had cut school lunch programs and other aid to the poor, outbreaks of diseases associated with poverty (such as tuberculosis) in America's inner cities were being documented in the scientific literature. From the footage shown on the TV news, it was apparent that those babies with AIDS were living in squalor, but as President Reagan had already pointed out—when he declared that catsup was a vegetable, at least for school lunch programs—they probably had all the catsup they needed.

At about the same time, the New York State Legislature was hearing testimony from leaders in the fight against AIDS. One of the most frequently quoted statements the media used in its coverage came from GMHC's executive director, Mel Rosen, who said that

AIDS was a speeding train heading for the American population. The possibility of AIDS being spread by casual contact and the image of a plague coming toward Americans like a steaming locomotive exploded across the air waves as Americans became transfixed.

The media were in high gear. Wages paid to film crews were increased to "combat duty" as they fanned out across the city in search of the most disfigured AIDS patients. The new disease was depicted on prime-time TV with the most gruesome footage of frail, skeletal patients covered in lesions. Despite the absence of supporting evidence in the scientific literature, Americans were thrown into a state of panic over an unfounded fear as five thousand copies of our safe sex booklet, *How to Have Sex in an Epidemic: One Approach,* were rolling off the presses, featuring a chapter on how to have sex safely with AIDS patients! After nearly a year in our support group, we couldn't shy away from confronting that reality, but it was a jarring juxtaposition to the frenzy breaking out all around us.

What was intended as an article for a gay ghetto press was about to be transformed into a manifesto that would find an extraordinary life outside the gay world and go on to define an epoch.

⇐ ⇒

Even though the precise ways in which AIDS was being transmitted had not yet been established, there was an understanding about the risks of specific sexual acts. Those that involved the exchange of body fluids seemed to carry the highest risks. It was commonly accepted from what doctors were observing, particularly in practices similar to Sonnabend's, where a history existed between doctors and their long-time patients, that receptive anal intercourse was the most dangerous sexual act. Whereas the proponents of the single-virus theory argued that it would only take a single, unlucky contact to contract AIDS (the popular analogy was that sex was now a game of Russian roulette and the new virus was the bullet), the multifactorial theory suggested that it was unlikely that a single exposure could result in full-blown AIDS and therefore, a single broken condom wouldn't be lethal. Condoms can and do break from time to time, and that's why organizations like GMHC, the Centers for Disease Control, and the American Foundation for AIDS Research did not produce any coherent safer sex recommendations. In fact, they actively opposed those of us who produced these recommendations with our own resources.

Safe sex was never—and could never—have been proposed in the terrifying early years by those who believed that if you had one broken condom you were dead. It was therefore left to the multifactorialists to invent safe sex. But because the theory from which safe sex was born was so despised by the gay leadership, it became the responsibility of ourselves, Dr. Sonnabend, Michael Callen, and me, to produce and disseminate the first safe sex guidelines, in the spring of 1983. Tragically, as a result of ongoing hostilities, it wasn't until 1985 that safe sex education began on a large scale in New York City, home to half the epidemic in America. What was even more tragic was that both sides of the debate had a piece of the truth but no one tried to reach out and find common ground.

Our booklet, *How to Have Sex in an Epidemic: One Approach,* was based on a model that attributed importance to all sexually transmitted infections, and proposed guidelines on how to prevent them. The multifactorial theory lost the debate on the cause of AIDS. But even if HIV causes AIDS, it is now well demonstrated that other infections, including sexually transmitted infections, increase HIV's infectivity as well as infectability by HIV, and they also promote disease progression. But today, some HIV-infected individuals have abandoned safe sex, believing, as many people do, that safe sex is just about HIV and AIDS. Nevertheless, preventing other sexually transmitted diseases remains important to the health of everyone, particularly HIV-positive people.

Although the community debate was essentially over, hostilities lingered. But there was no stopping an idea whose time had come, no matter how hard some people tried.

In the same month that our booklet came out, Mathilde Krim, PhD, joined Dr. Sonnabend in establishing a foundation to support his research. Krim had been a colleague of Sonnabend's in the 1960s when they were involved in interferon-related research. Krim's husband, Arthur, was the leading Democratic fundraiser in Hollywood and head of Orion Pictures. When she began arriving in her limousine at Dr. Sonnabend's office on West 12th Street, Callen called her the gay community's fairy godmother; and for a moment it did seem like Billie Burke was magically descending over Munchkinland. Callen had just given a powerful speech before the New York Legislature that began his rise to one of the most visible and effective AIDS activists America would ever know. We were hired to do safe sex education for the new foundation, but when word got out, GMHC representatives demanded to see her and the day after that, Callen and I were let go. Krim thought she had come to help a beleaguered community in crisis; what she discovered were some bitter, divisive factions. Different people have different recollections of that time, but I have a collection of inspiring and encouraging letters from her lauding my work on safe sex over the years and urging me to look more broadly to include women, which I regret that I was quite late in doing.

But in our weekly support group meetings, bonds were solid among men who understood exactly what we were trying to do, and they became our fiercest allies. When our safe sex education efforts were blocked, the entire group joined forces and created the first safe sex education campaign in New York City; it was moving to see gravely ill men working to help others avoid their fate. But as soon as we had plastered posters and planted brochures at every bathhouse and sex club, from Harlem to Wall Street, the *Native* vigorously attacked the campaign and business owners seized it as an excuse to make all the materials disappear.

GMHC's director of education, Federico Gonzales, called Callen with an offer to buy all 5,000 copies of our pamphlet on one condition, that references to the debate over whether AIDS was caused by a single exposure to a new virus or resulted from multiple factors would be excised from the booklet. We declined. As a result, New York City, home to half of all the U.S. AIDS cases, would not have its first safe sex education campaign for two unendurable years. Funding panels often included one or more of our former sparring partners. Our grant proposals were repeatedly rejected. Our three-man collaboration was nearing an end.

I had lugged cartons of pamphlets to conferences and bookstores, filled order requests, and mailed copies all over the world. Someone listed *How to Have Sex in an Epidemic* in a national library index. A gay man working at Barnes and Noble on 8th Street in Greenwich Village put our measly-looking pamphlet in the window display. Soon, our little booklet-that-could was being mentioned in publications that ran the gamut from highbrow intellectual *(The New York Review of Books)* to grunge-pit sleaze *(DungeonMaster)*. But the most substantial exposure in a national, mainstream publication came from articles written by Celia Farber for *SPIN,* the first and, for a long time, the only in-depth coverage that mentioned the three of us and went into detail about how safe sex came about. Michael Callen adored her, as do I, but with a tinge of sadness: for nearly a decade, a mid-twenties heterosexual woman gave more coverage to the invention of safe sex than did all the gay media in America combined.

Twenty years later, with condom ads running frequently on MTV, it seems like such a no-brainer: Why would safe sex have to be invented when it's just common sense to use condoms for protection against AIDS and other sexually transmitted infections?

But that was not the case at the onset of the disease. In the 1970s, condoms were a quaint remnant from a bygone era; sales had plummeted. With the increasing birth control options for women that helped launch the sexual revolution, condoms fell out of favor. Gay men, with no concern about pregnancy, felt certain that there would always be a pill or shot to cure whatever consequences resulted from sex. In the 1979 movie *Looking for Mr. Goodbar*, Diane Keaton plays Theresa, a sexually active woman. In one memorable scene, she's about to have sex with a conservative-minded man. When he takes out a condom, she almost can't believe it. Like most sexually active women of the day, Theresa is on birth control and astounded by the novelty of seeing a condom. In a fit of hysterical laughter, she tears the wrapper open and blows it up like a balloon. Condoms had become a joke. We in the audience laughed along in recognition. This was the fertile ground for AIDS.

When we published *How to Have Sex in an Epidemic: One Approach* in the spring of 1983, it was absolutely radical in a time of absolute terror. Our mode of distribution was my two feet, carrying copies to bookstores around the city, while on the newsstands *New York* magazine's cover story, "AIDS ANXIETY," accurately captured life in Manhattan this way:

> The number of [AIDS] cases is doubling every six months. As of May, there were 722 cases in this city. . . . 72 percent were male homosexuals. Another 17 percent were IV drug users. Just 4 percent were Haitians. And 1 percent were hemophiliacs. . . . Dr. James Oleske received a call asking if it was risky to invite a homosexual relative to a christening. . . . 100 inmates at Rikers Island went on a hunger strike demanding that all homosexuals be banned from the kitchen. . . . At the Bureau of Preventable Disease, the telephone began ringing as many as 50 times a day with inquiries from fearful citizens. One

caller wanted reassurance that mosquitoes are not known to carry AIDS. Another was told there was no reason to fire a maid simply because she is Haitian. One doctor was stopped by a neighbor who wanted to know if it was still safe to visit Greenwich Village. Another neighbor asked if she should worry about working with a homosexual. . . . On Long Island, a woman confided to a close friend that her husband had come down with AIDS. Suddenly, none of the neighbors wanted their children to play with the woman's daughter. The friend pressured the woman to take her daughter out of school. The sanitation men refused to pick up the woman's garbage. . . . After being diagnosed, one 24-year-old patient was driven from his family's home and left to live on the street. When one patient died, his family refused to claim the body. AIDS victims have been fired from their jobs, driven from their homes, and deserted by their loved ones. Any homosexual . . . has become an object of dread. New York in 1983 has become a place where a woman telephones Montefiore Medical Center and asks if her children should wear gloves on the subway.

And I'm going store to store asking merchants if they'd like to have a few copies to sell on consignment of a booklet called *How to Have Sex in an Epidemic: One Approach.*

In the midst of all-out hysteria over contagion, our booklet said, "Suck, but don't let your partner come in your mouth," because we had a theory to base it on. And twenty years later, our guidelines are still being widely followed. That was why we wanted a debate, not just so sex could be seen in a rational way, but so that life could, too. But the real debate kept being drowned out. And no one paid a higher price for that than gay men themselves.

In the fall of 1984, local TV news shows started reporting on continued activity in New York City sex clubs; finally, a group formed to create a safe sex education campaign. Nearly two years after we published our booklet, New York's "Great Sex Is Healthy Sex" safe sex campaign, which was *How to Have Sex in Epidemic*'s guidelines with a no-poppers stand added, was cynically launched to save our sex clubs when TV crews came snooping. I was working full time as a driver for the Red Cross, taking inner-city AIDS patients to their medical appointments when the final grant to get funding for me to work on safe sex was turned down. Car driver was not what I wanted to contribute to AIDS, but my CNN appearance had paid off: a doctor who kept Kosher and observed the Sabbath asked me to move into his oceanfront high-rise in Florida.

I hoped that, in a year or two, opportunities for safe sex education might improve in New York. They certainly were making their mark in many places around the world. As I left Manhattan behind, I was finally able to feel a moment of accomplishment that my work had contributed to an idea that was taking hold of people's consciousness and carried the potential to empower ordinary people.

In Florida, I read pro-sex feminist books on the beach by day, dined as a wealthy doctor's spouse by night, and slept under the stars on a spacious balcony till dawn. A Miami newspaper dubbed me a "safe sex missionary" after Miami's Jack Campbell, owner of the Club Bath Chain and inventor of the modern gay bathhouse, hired me to give safe sex lectures in South Florida bathhouses. The age of condoms had arrived: Gay men were using them, appreciating them and adapting to them well.

A joyful year as a high-class beach bum only delayed the inevitable. You guessed it: Back in New York City, I became the first escort to advertise safe sex in the *Advocate*. Immediately, the floodgates opened and dozens of ads followed suit. Even in the third grade I had loved being a trendsetter, but this time I brought safe sex out of the closet in a way "Healthy Sex Is Great Sex" (puh-leez) never could. As thanks, a client installed a sling and soundproofed one of my rooms. I had returned to my calling, but it was mainly to support my writing. Michael Callen wanted me to write a book celebrating our involvement in the invention of safe sex (after I had refused to let him install surveillance cameras in my playroom as a safe sex education tool). Condoms had finally become the norm.

⇚   ⇛

But in time, personal and political agendas moved in to undermine safe sex. A number of those who stepped forward to help out in the AIDS crisis had intentions that were good for some people but harmful for others. They saw AIDS as a bully pulpit to get gay men to settle down into monogamy. When it seemed like many gay men wouldn't listen, confusion was created in order to undermine their confidence in safe sex. This was achieved by gleaning "scientific facts" from preliminary or questionable studies to foster an atmosphere of uncertainty. These unhelpful helpers would then ask, How could anyone doubt conclusions of studies appearing in "respected" scientific journals? How could non-experts deny this growing body of contradictory findings that "proved" no one could say for certain what safe sex really was? Do you want to risk your life while the jury is still out? What about the life of your partner?

Another contingent was embarrassed and squeamish about mentioning anal sex, especially in mixed company. They felt that we should do it but not talk about it. They wanted to use the spotlight from AIDS to show Americans that gay men were just as normal as the rest of the happy, well-adjusted, heterosexual majority. With its constant emphasis on unprotected, receptive anal intercourse as the highest risk for acquiring AIDS, safe sex threatened to leave a stain on their suit-and-tie appeal to America.

There never has been much disagreement that it is the receptive, not the insertive, partner who bears the risk for the transmission of HIV and AIDS, and since there have always been approximately four times as many male cases of AIDS as female cases in the United States, it's strange that no one seems to understand what that says about the men.

Safe sex began as a simple concept that didn't demand much: "don't get sperm inside your rectum," and later when cases of AIDS among women began to rise, "don't get sperm inside your vagina" (although the risk in vaginal intercourse has never been as great as in receptive anal intercourse, the risk is still there).

In 1996, to mark the fifteenth year of the AIDS epidemic, much of the gay press around the country published feature articles highlighting achievements since the epidemic began. None I scoured, not even national magazines devoted exclusively to AIDS, bothered to mention safe sex. The anti-sex forces within our own ranks had claimed a lot of ground and gay men had become demoralized trying to defend it against what Callen called "dueling studies." On an assignment for *SPIN,* I discovered instances where safe sex education was just a way to generate paperwork in order to justify funding.

More and more gay men I knew were either giving up on safe sex or no longer felt they had to lie about not doing it. Peer pressure was waning fast. There was now enough published research so that anyone from Jerry Falwell to the most ardent AIDS activist could cite scientific studies to back up whatever they wanted to argue. Safe sex was getting lost in a blizzard of confusion and uncertainty. Gay men were demoralized and feeling a sense of betrayal that no one seemed able or motivated to articulate or analyze. And so unsafe sex returned with a pent-up rage.

Epilogue

Safe sex is as simple as a celibacy campaign and a hell of a lot more fun—but infection with HIV is still lethal, and celibacy is not. There is still no vaccine despite nineteen years of promises. The cornerstone of safe sex is knowing that it still is a matter of life and death for sexually active women and, even more so, for sexually active gay men who engage in receptive anal intercourse.

The most wonderful thing about safe sex is that it keeps you healthy for a longer time to enjoy even more sex and have even more fun. Then one day, when you meet someone special who makes you feel more complete and happier than you've ever known, experience has made you rich and you have a healthy body to share as well. Safe sex offers protection for more than HIV; it greatly reduces the chances of getting a long, annoying list of other sexually transmitted infections.

Safe sex is for people who know to think long term, who understand that the world often appears on the brink of disaster but somehow tomorrow comes. From my work in AIDS activism and safe sex education, I've known hundreds of people who died from AIDS and complications from AIDS, and not one ever said it was worth it. More than a few pleaded with me to write this book to warn the next generation, to urge a healthy skepticism of what advice is being offered and what evidence supports it. You should ask questions. Are there any other opinions? What are they? What evidence supports them? Verify what is said and get a broad range opinions. Be suspicious of those who refuse to explain their view or produce evidence for scrutiny. Be aware that it is easy for those with knowledge to abuse the trust of those without knowledge.

You can always count on any issue that involves sex to bring out the zealots of all kinds in droves. But they mustn't distract us from staying focused on the two overwhelming risks for the sexual transmission of HIV: unprotected receptive vaginal intercourse and, to a greater degree, receptive anal intercourse. And remember, dear reader, to do something to spread the message, and not just on a one-to-one basis.

The two most important discoveries of the sexual revolution of the 1960s and 1970s are the two most important sexual pleasures that safe sex was invented to protect and that effective safe sex education must target: anal orgasms and clitoral orgasms—neither of which are greatly hindered by the use of a condom. These are the heart and soul of making safe sex work for you. There are psychological and emotional reasons why people don't like using condoms. But we must not let that obscure the fact that condoms do not significantly decrease the physical pleasure of two overwhelming risks. AIDS has taught gay men something women have always known: it is the receptive partner in sex who bears the greatest burden of consequences from sex. Can we care enough about ourselves to demand our partner respects our lives? Because, the truth is, whenever someone tells you they don't like using condoms, they are telling you that they are a risk for sexually transmitted infections. And sexually transmitted infections not only increase HIV's infectivity, but also infectability by HIV. The only way to get around condoms for sexually active women and gay men is oral sex, for which the risk for HIV infection in healthy people is negligible. Yes, sex is about merging, it's about skin to skin, but in the age of AIDS, use kissing and oral sex for "merging" and protect yourself during intercourse. That's what was argued, under the scientific supervision of Dr. Joseph Sonnabend, in our May 1983 safe sex manifesto.

As author Edward King stated in his book, *Safety in Numbers: Safer Sex and Gay Men,* "It was *How to Have Sex in an Epidemic: One Approach* which pioneered the approach to safer sex which we recognize today. . . . By deducing a means by which gay men could continue to 'have sex in an epidemic' but take rational precautions to make that sex safer, *How to Have Sex in an Epidemic* provided the model for safer sex campaigns . . . ever since."[1]

It is a tragedy that sexually active gay men and women have been led to believe that safe sex is just about HIV. It's about self-esteem. It's about character. It's about having a sense of community and caring for your partner. It's about sexually transmitted diseases. And it's about being armed with the knowledge necessary to make your own informed choices.

This has been the history of my involvement in safe sex. I hope others write more stories and make more history.

Appendix

How to Have Sex
in an Epidemic:
One Approach

(Originally published in 1983)

"Any disease that is treated as a mystery and acutely enough feared will be felt to be morally, if not literally, contagious."

—Susan Sontag

Illness as Metaphor

"What do you get when you kiss a guy?
You get enough germs to catch pneumonia
After you do, he'll never phone 'ya
I'll never fall in love again.

—Hall David

Foreword

by Joseph A. Sonnabend, M.D.

Gay men living in cities where the epidemic of AIDS has struck the hardest have a tremendous need for information in order to make informed decisions regarding the extent and nature of their sexual activities. This pamphlet is addressed to those who agree that no good evidence exists for the casual spread of AIDS and that there is, in fact, substantial evidence against this.

It is clearly not the authors' intention to discourage those who have chosen to refrain from all sexual contact during this epidemic; neither is it in any way an encouragement of promiscuity. The authors recognize that there are those who might consider sexual activity too hazardous despite modifications designed to protect one from acquiring CMV and from exposure to semen, while at the same time recognizing that many gay men are continuing to have sex. It is to this latter group that the authors direct their recommendations.

The authors have not produced a guide for the prevention of all STDs. Rather, they explore the many different forms of sexual expression open to gay men and clearly present suggestions to prevent exposure to sperm and CMV (which are probably key factors in the development of AIDS).

In some ways, the tragedy of AIDS is bringing gay men closer together and many are looking for more enduring and loving relationships. Perhaps the most important message contained in this pamphlet is the authors' premise that when affection informs a sexual relationship, the motivation exists to find ways to protect each other from disease.

I wholeheartedly recommend this pamphlet to those wishing to find a path through the confusing and contradictory advice emanating from so many directions.

Preface

The question on every sexually active gay man's mind these days is: "How can I avoid AIDS?"

Since no one knows for sure how gay men are developing AIDS, you may wonder how rational guidelines to prevent the disease can be formulated. Obviously, we believe that such guidelines *can* be formulated, but it is important to bear in mind that the guidelines offered in this pamphlet are based on the particular theory regarding the cause of AIDS to which we subscribe. This means that we will have to briefly discuss the different theories about how AIDS develops in gay men, and we do so in detail.

Although we ourselves favor what is known as the multifactorial theory, it is important that you know that prevailing opinion appears to favor the view that a "new," as yet unidentified AIDS agent is most probably responsible for the disease in all affected groups.

The recommendations that we will propose are based on the multifactorial theory of AIDS in gay men. These guidelines are designed to teach you how to reduce your chances of exposure to CMV and other infections by suggesting ways to interrupt disease transmission.

And even if a new agent is ultimately discovered, these same guidelines may also reduce your risks even if a new virus is involved.

There are those for whom giving up sex would not be particularly difficult. For others, this would constitute a drastic reaction.

Some will respond to the worst possible scenario and avoid all sexual contact. Others may go so far as to avoid even casual, non-sexual contact with patients—perhaps even casual contact with healthy gay men.

The decision to respond in such an extreme fashion must be yours. If you have made the decision to become celibate, we have no wish to change your mind. However, if you have read this far, you probably belong to the group of men for whom such drastic measures would be warranted only if there were firm evidence supporting the existence of a highly contagious new AIDS agent. If you believe, as we do, that the evidence strongly suggests otherwise, read on.

Introduction

Today in most large urban centers, what began as sexual freedom has become a tyranny of sexually transmitted diseases. Some of the diseases which sexually active gay men have become all too familiar with include: gonorrhea, syphilis, proctitis, urethritis and shigellosis; amoebiasis, giardiasis and venereal warts; hepatitis A, hepatitis B, hepatitis non-A/non-B; mononucleosis; oral and genital herpes; and lymphogranuloma venereum.

Added to this long list are two other serious epidemics which we believe are related: Cytomegalovirus (CMV) and Acquired Immune Deficiency Syndrome (AIDS).

Finding ways to have sex and avoid these epidemics might seem impossible, but we believe it's not. This pamphlet offers advice on one means of reducing (and hopefully eliminating) risk which has yet to receive proper attention: *limiting what sex acts you choose to perform to ones which interrupt disease transmission.* The advantage of this approach is that if you avoid taking in your partner(s)' body fluids, you will better protect yourself not only from most serious diseases but also from many of the merely inconvenient ones. The key to this approach is modifying what you do—not how often you do it nor with how many different partners.

In the end, how you have sex is a matter of personal choice. But in the age of AIDS, it is important to realize that each one of us is now betting his life on what changes we do or do not make.

As you read on, we hope we make at least one point clear: Sex doesn't make you sick—diseases do. Gay sex doesn't make you sick—gay men who are sick do. Once you understand how diseases are transmitted, you can begin to explore medically safe sex.

Our challenge is to figure out how we can have gay, life-affirming sex, satisfy our emotional needs, and stay alive!

1

What Causes Aids?

There are two general theories under serious discussion at the moment: the "new" agent theory and the multifactorial theory.

The New Agent Theory: Some researchers believe that the cause of AIDS is a new AIDS agent, presumably a virus, which attacks the immune system and which is the common link between all of the groups at risk (Haitian entrants, I/V drug abusers, hemophiliacs and infants of high risk groups who are also victims of poverty). This theory proposes that this putative new killer virus has been introduced into the gay male community and is being spread by sexual contact. Some propose that even a single exposure to this virus will produce AIDS after a long incubation period.

The Multifactorial Theory: Other researchers believe that a number of different factors must occur in order for AIDS to develop. Rather than occurring after a single exposure, this theory suggests that the syndrome "builds up" over a period of continued exposure to sperm containing large amounts of cytomegalovirus (CMV). CMV is a common virus and has long been recognized as a cause of diseases in many different settings. It can also be carried by people who are in apparent good heatlh.

What is the evidence for the "New" Virus theory? The argument in favor of the new agent theory rests on the appearance of a similar syndrome occurring in each of the risk groups listed above. Hypothetically, a disease resulting from a single agent transmitted by sexual contact and by blood could link these groups. Hepatitis B, for example, is spread in such a way and occurs more frequently in gay men and people who receive blood transfusions than in the "general" population. But it's important to remember that it is an *assumption* that what is being labeled as "AIDS" in each risk group is in fact the same disease.

Added to the assumption that the disease is the same in each group is the further assumption that the disease is *new* in each group and that it develops in the same way. Just because a disease is newly recognized does not necessarily mean that the disease is new. Many different agents are known to cause disturbances in the function of the immune system. Thus, one must be cautious in presuming that the appearance of similar diseases in different groups is occurring for the same reasons. Stated simply, although the pathways to immune suppression are many and varied, once a person becomes immunosuppressed, the diseases one encounters may be the same.

Thus, what is being labeled as "AIDS" may not actually be developing in the same way in each of the different groups.

Nevertheless, several viruses have been proposed as being responsible for the epidemic. These include a human T-cell leukemia virus (HTLV) later renamed HIV and the African Swine Fever Virus (ASFV). However, HTLV has not been uniformly identified in all AIDS patients and it is possible that the presence of antibodies to HTLV is a *result,* rather than a *cause,* of the underlying immune deficiency. Studies on ASFV have yet to be done. Even if antibodies to ASFV are discovered in some AIDS patients, it is likely that this too will prove to be a virus that affects individuals who are already immunosuppressed.

Although it would be economical to evoke a "new" agent to account for AIDS in each of the groups, the facts remain that in the three years since AIDS in gay men was first recognized:

1. No "new" virus has been shown to play a causative role in the disease;
2. Attempts to replicate AIDS in animals by injecting them with the blood and other body fluids of AIDS patients have all failed; and
3. Not a single health care worker has developed AIDS solely from patient contact.

In summary, no firm evidence has been produced to support the view that a new virus is the cause of AIDS nor that the disease can be "spread" by casual contact.

What is the evidence for the "Multifactorial" theory?   The multifactorial theory of AIDS proposes that the key links in AIDS in gay men are repeated infection with CMV against a backdrop of mild immuneosuppression caused by exposure to sperm. But, you may say, surely gay men have been exposed to their partners' sperm since the beginning of time. And since CMV is not a new virus, why would AIDS be occurring in gay men *now*?

To answer the pressing question of "Why now?", the multifactorial theory proposes that the *new* element in sexually active urban gay men is the shocking high *prevalence* of CMV among sexually active urban gay men. Instead of proposing a new virus, the multifactorial theory proposes that there is simply a lot more of an old virus.

Evidence suggests that the number of sexually active urban gay men carrying CMV has increased dramatically over the last decade. One New York City study has shown that as many as one out of every four sexually active gay men are capable of infecting their sexual partners with CMV in 1983.

Oversimplified, the multifactorial theory proposes that since you may be multiply and repeatedly infected with CMV, AIDS in gay men may be the result of the body's inability to free itself from these repeated CMV infections.

In this theory, AIDS is seen as *developing* over a period of time rather than spreading from a single contact in the classic sense of contagion.

In addition to repeated infection with CMV, other significant factors which we believe may be involved in the development of AIDS in gay men include the immunosuppressive effects of being exposed to the sperm of many different partners and the harmful effects of immune complexes.

Immune complexes are combinations of antibodies and the agent that stimulated the formation of the antibody in the first place. Immune complexes are not normally found in the blood of healthy individuals. Unfortunately, the lifestyle of a sexually active urban gay man can expose him to many different factors which produce immune complexes. For example, immune complexes occur on exposure to sperm and they have also been associated with hepatitis B, syphilis, CMV and possibly even gonorrhea.

So back to the question: "How can I avoid AIDS?" Theories are only theories; what changes should you make? What risks can you afford to take?

As many have pointed out in the age of AIDS, all life involves some risk.

The advice in this paper is based on interrupting disease transmission, in particular transmission of CMV. In addition, our advice will help you to avoid sperm and its added immunosuppressive burden.

Whether the cause of AIDS is a new agent or many common agents, this paper will show you how to substantially reduce or even eliminate the means by which any such agent or agents might be transmitted from one person to another. Simply put, the advice in this paper is based on what we *do* know about diseases—not what we *don't* know.

2

What You Should Know
about CMV

As we have stated, we believe that CMV is the "trigger" causing AIDS in gay men. But even if the link between repeated CMV infections and AIDS is ultimately disproven, it is still crucial for sexually active gay men to learn about CMV since a single CMV infection can cause serious illness.

Although most gay men know little about CMV, major epidemics of CMV are being documented among sexually active gay men in New York and San Francisco. Many researchers believe that similar epidemics of CMV are occurring in the other cities reporting most of the AIDS cases in gay men.

1. CMV is excreted in the body fluids: saliva, blood, urine, sperm (and possibly seminal fluid). Exposure to sweat is probably not a significant risk for CMV.
2. The highest concentration of CMV is found in sperm and urine.
3. The concentration of viruses in a particular exposure can affect your chances of actually contracting the infection. Massive inoculations with CMV, such as would occur through rectal exposure to infected sperm, could overwhelm the body's natural ability to fight off the infection.
4. CMV is one of five different herpes viruses and can remain in your system for life after the initial infection. Like other herpes viruses, this latent CMV infection can be reactivated in immunosuppressed patients.
5. CMV appears to be one common link found in all gay men with AIDS. CMV has been found in the tumors of gay

men with Kaposi's sarcoma. Some researchers believe that Epstein-Barr virus (which may be reactivated by CMV) probably explains the high incidence of lymphomas among gay men with AIDS and may also be one of the causes of lymphadenopathy.

6. A CMV infection usually causes flu-like symptoms. Some CMV infections may be mild and go unnoticed. These are called asymptomatic CMV infections. Other CMV infections can be serious enough to require hospitalization.

7. If you get a CMV infection you may be contagious *FOR OVER A YEAR.* Even if you have no obvious symptoms, you may be "shedding" or "excreting" the virus in your sperm for over a year. Though you may not realize it, it is not safe to continue having the kind of sexual contacts which might infect your partners. Also, since your CMV infection has weakened your body's ability to fight off other infections properly, you place yourself at greater risk for contracting other diseases.

8. If you discover that you have or had a CMV infection, do not panic. Having a CMV infection does not necessarily mean you will develop AIDS. Close to 100% of all sexually active urban gay men tested have had a CMV infection by the age of 30. (In one study, the comparable figure in sexually active heterosexuals was 54%.) According to the multifactorial theory, the risk for AIDS is *repeated* CMV infection.

9. One out of every four sexually active urban gay men is likely to be contagious for one or more strains of CMV. The gay men in the New York City study were a random group. The CMV excretion rate might well have been even higher than one in four if highly promiscuous gay men had been studied. (In sexually active heterosexuals in one San Francisco study, the comparable figure was one out of every 20.) The shockingly high levels of CMV

excretion may be the "new" element which explains why
AIDS is occurring *now* as opposed to 10 years ago (when,
presumably, CMV rates were much lower).

10. Since the highest concentration of CMV is in sperm, rectal
intercourse would permit a massive inoculation with
CMV. Rectal exposure to CMV is probably the most hazardous.

How Can I Find Out If I Am Contagious for CMV?

The only definitive test for CMV is to culture the virus from urine, semen
and blood (and possibly from saliva). In addition to virus isolation, it is ad-
visable to test the blood for antibody levels to CMV. The IgG antibody
tests detect whether you have ever had CMV infection; the IgM antibody
test indicates a recent or current infection.

A complete battery of CMV testing would consist of both virus cultures and antibody tests and may cost about $200. Unfortunately, these
tests have not been easily obtainable.

Private physicians should be encouraged to arrange for these tests either by contacting medical centers or determining which private labs do
these tests (not all do). Arranging for these tests will require some effort
on the part of your physician and obviously are expensive.

But for two people who meet and want to become lovers and who
wish to ensure that they are healthy from the beginning of their relationship, this battery of CMV tests (in addition to routine VD and amoeba
testing) would be a good investment. Once both partners are assured that
each is free from CMV and other infections, they need not take most of
the precautions that we will outline in this pamphlet since these precautions ware designed to interrupt the transmission of CMV and other infections. Of course, remaining free from CMV and other diseases will
depend on not exposing oneself to infection.

As with all laboratory testing, tests which attempt to culture CMV
from sperm and urine cannot be guaranteed to be 100% accurate since
CMV may be excreted intermittently. However, the antibody test, combined with attempts to isolate the virus should help to clarify the question
of contagion.

Fortunately, efforts are under way to make tests for CMV quicker, cheaper and more readily available.

The Effects of CMV and Sperm on Your Immune System

The AIDS crisis has focused a lot of attention on our immune systems. What is our body's immune system and how does it work?

The immune system is one of the body's defenses against infections. To oversimplify, when your body encounters a virus, bacteria or parasite, your immune system "recognizes" it as "foreign" and begins to mount an attack. Antibodies and other substances are formed within the body to direct the various systems to attack the foreign agent. Cells are mobilized to destroy infected cells.

A number of different factors affect how well your immune system responds to an attack. For example, drug abuse, poor diet, stress, genetic factors, chemotherapy, increasing age and even overexposure to ultraviolet light impair to various degrees your body's ability to respond properly.

In addition, some infections themselves weaken your body's ability to mount an effective response to other infections. The strain which multiple infections place on the immune system is one element of what may be occurring in AIDS.

Recently, it has been shown that the introduction into the rectum of sperm from many different partners can result in immunological changes that may provide a background of immune suppression which could adversely affect the body's response to CMV and other infectious agents. Clearly these harmful effects of sperm have not in themselves caused obvious health problems. People have enjoyed fucking each other throughout history without ill effect. But the combination of sperm-induced immune defects together with repeated reinfection with CMV and other factors constitutes a major attack on your immune system.

How to Determine Your Risk for CMV

Determining your chances for contracting CMV (and most other STDs) will be a function of three interrelated factors:

1. The NUMBER of DIFFERENT sexual partners you have.

2. The number of these different partners WHO ARE CON-
   TAGIOUS FOR CMV; and
3. WHICH SPECIFIC SEX ACTS YOU PERFORM that are
   capable of transmitting CMV.

Ethics and Responsibility

Before we examine specific sexual acts for their risk for CMV, a few words
about sexual responsibility are in order. Since we are a community, taking
responsibility for our *own* health during sex ultimately requires that we
protect our *partners* health as well as our own.

When you are deciding what sexual acts will take place, you must
not only ask "Will this pose a health risk to me?", but also: "Will this pose
a health risk to my partner?"

In all recommendations which follow, it is vital to the survival of
each member of the sexually active gay community that the issues of your
own health and the health of your partner(s) never become separated.

The precautions you will need to take in order to protect yourself
from getting CMV or any other infection will depend on what sexual acts
you prefer. Safeguarding your own health means you must plan ahead of
time what you will do, how you can do it safely and what items (like rubbers) you might need to have available. PLAN AHEAD!

Staying in Control

Staying in control of what you do is the key to this approach to medically
safe sex. In the heat of passion it's easy to throw caution to the wind. But
if you finally become sick of getting sick, it should become easier to stay
in control.

Discussing precautions before you have sex might seem like a turn
off, but if you enjoy staying healthy, you may eventually come to eroticize
whatever precautions you require prior to the sexual encounter.

If the man of your dreams starts dragging you out of your favorite
cruise bar, you must be especially cautious and guarded. Don't let yourself
get into situations where temptation may get the better of you. Simply
stated, if you can't resist rimming, be sure your head is never within strik-
ing distance.

Safe sex requires that you be sober. Alcohol, poppers and other recreational drugs can impair your decision-making abilities. Gauge yourself honestly.

Selecting Your Partner: The Importance of Talking

Decide ahead of time that your partner must respect your health concerns. Some of the hottest men you meet may have their heads buried in the sand when it comes to protecting their health (not to mention your health). But since worrying about disease (or death) during or after sex simply has to be affecting everyone's enjoyment, you may be able to convince your partners to stop denying the reality of disease and to join you in finding ways to have sex which will protect you both. Demonstrating a concern for healthy sex may even make you more appealing!

Learning to Estimate Risk

The advice in this pamphlet is based on interrupting the transmission of cytomegalovirus. There are three reasons for this.

First, if you believe CMV plays a role in the development of AIDS, then these measures will prevent exposure to the virus and reduce your risk for AIDS.

Second, if a new, as-yet-unidentified virus is responsible for AIDS, the measures proposed to prevent CMV transmission are likely to be effective in preventing the spread of any such virus. If such a new agent exists, it is clearly not infectious by casual contact since there have been no cases of AIDS among individuals taking care of patients. Therefore, transmission of such an agent by sweat or by air-borne droplet exposure would seem improbable.

Third, even if CMV does not contribute to the development of AIDS, it still is capable of causing serious illness.

THIS IS *NOT* A VD PREVENTION MANUAL. We are speaking about CMV and AIDS. Please always keep in mind that there *are* diseases which can be spread by mere body contact: syphilis and herpes are but two examples. We urge you to consult one of the many useful VD pamphlets.

With CMV, it is easy to estimate your own risk. Simply ask yourself: "If I perform this particular sex act, will I take in my partner's body fluids?

If so, is there any way I can reduce or eliminate this risk to me and to my partner?"

The importance of cleanliness is obvious. In settings such as backrooms, where your partner may have had multiple partners and where you must assume he has had no opportunity to wash up properly, your risk for diseases such as amoebiasis will obviously be high.

Now we will examine specific sexual acts and teach you to estimate your and your partner's risk. Remember, in the examples that follow, we are primarily examining your risk for a specific virus—CMV.

Sucking

Unfortunately, sucking your partner cannot be made risk free (unless your partner is wearing a rubber!). Since the highest concentration of CMV is carried in sperm (and urine), swallowing a load of come can be a massive inoculation of CMV.

If you want to REDUCE your risk of getting CMV, suck—but don't let your partner come in your mouth. This will substantially reduce your risk for CMV. (No one knows for sure, but it seems possible that CMV may be carried in low concentrations in the seminal fluid (pre-come) which precedes orgasm.)

If your partner "accidentally" comes in your mouth or if you get a taste of pre-come fluid, spitting it out will probably reduce your risk for CMV.

REMEMBER:

1. Sucking is a moderate risk for CMV.
2. If you suck, you can reduce your risk for CMV by preventing your partner from coming in your mouth.
3. If your partner accidentally comes in your mouth (or if you taste pre-come fluid), reduce your risk by spitting it out.
4. Apart from CMV, sucking can of course transmit other diseases such as syphilis and gonorrhea and in certain settings amoebas.

Getting Sucked

Getting sucked by your partner probably poses no risk to you of contracting CMV since you are not taking in any of your partner's body fluids. However, since you are concerned about protecting your partner's health, protect him from CMV—DON'T COME IN HIS MOUTH.

REMEMBER:

1. Getting sucked probably poses no risk to you for CMV, but is a risk to your partner if you are contagious for CMV and if you come in his mouth.
2. For your partner's sake, make sure you wash before sex.
3. Apart from CMV, you could still get other diseases such as herpes simplex and syphilis if your partner is contagious for any of these infections.

Fucking

Fucking someone also probably poses no risk to you of contracting CMV since it is unlikely that your partner's body fluids will be absorbed through the urethra of your penis.

Unless you're absolutely certain that you aren't contagious for CMV, protect your partner from CMV by always using a rubber. If you cannot adjust to rubbers, the next best thing is to limit your partner's risk by pulling out before you come. A compromise might be to fuck without a rubber until you feel yourself close to coming and then put on a rubber before you shoot.

Getting used to rubbers might take some time, but stick with it.

Be aware that rubbers are not designed for assholes and might rip apart during penetration.

If you are using a rubber, hold onto it at the base when you pull out of your partner in order to prevent leakage of sperm and to prevent the rubber from sliding off inside your partner.

REMEMBER:

1. Fucking someone probably poses no risk to you for CMV.

2. Protect your partner's chances of exposure to CMV by wearing a rubber.

3. If you aren't wearing a rubber and you aren't sure whether you're contagious for CMV, never come inside your partner's ass.

4. When wearing a rubber, check before you come to make sure that your rubber hasn't slipped off.

5. If you're using a rubber, make sure that it stays on while you're pulling out of your partner after you've come.

6. Again, apart from CMV, other STDs can be transmitted to you through fucking.

Getting Fucked

Getting fucked poses a great risk to you if your partner is contagious for CMV and comes inside you when he's not wearing a rubber. Evidence suggests that gay men who have been fucked by many different men are at a higher risk for developing AIDS (and many other STDs) than those who primarily engage in other sexual practices.

Because of the ridiculous and dangerous stereotype that being "passive" and getting fucked are somehow "unmanly," some gay men tend to be defensive about any warnings concerning the medical hazards of anal passivity. Remember that the issue is disease—not sex. The risk isn't the act of getting fucked; the risk is getting exposed to CMV and the sperm of many different partners. It is an unfortunate biological fact that passive rectal intercourse is one of the most dangerous sexual activities from a disease transmission standpoint. This is so because:

1. Sperm generally contains the highest concentrations of CMV which your partner may be "shedding";

2. The inner lining of your asshole is easily penetrated by infectious agents;

3. Unlike infections which occur outside your body, an infection in your rectum may go unnoticed for long periods of time; and

4. Sperm itself introduced rectally probably produces more harmful immune responses than if introduced by mouth.

CMV carried in your partner's sperm might pass directly into your bloodstream through the mucosa which line your asshole. The only protection between you and CMV is a thin layer of body fluid which may be washed away by douching. If your partner is willing to wear a rubber, douching in moderation is up to you.

The best way to protect yourself from CMV (and many other STDs) while getting fucked is to provide your partner with a rubber and encourage him to use it.

If your partner just can't adjust to rubbers, you may substantially reduce your risk for CMV by making sure your partner doesn't come inside you. A compromise might be to let your partner fuck you without a rubber and make sure that he either pulls out or puts a rubber on before he comes.

REMEMBER:

1. Getting fucked without a rubber is the highest risk for CMV.
2. Unless you're certain that your partner is not excreting CMV, provide your partner with a rubber and encourage him to use it.
3. If your partner won't use a rubber, make sure he pulls out before coming or see that he puts the rubber on just before he comes.
4. Avoid excessive douching.

No Risk Sex

In terms of CMV, no risk sex is sex which does not involve taking in each other's body fluids. You can virtually eliminate risk for CMV by limiting your sexual contact to: (1) creative masturbation; and (2) creative penetration. As always, keep your hands away from your mouth until you have washed.

Creative Masturbation offers alternatives to jerking off alone at home. These include: mutual masturbation, group J/O, body contact, fantasy, dirty talk (verbal), voyeurism, exhibitionism, touching, fingers (not fists), titplay, toys, etc.

Creative Penetration includes the use of condoms, fingers (not hands) and "toys."

REMEMBER: Merely touching your partner's body poses no risk for CMV, but touching may still involve risk for those infections such as herpes simplex or syphilis which can be transmitted by mere body contact.

Kissing

Kissing poses a moderate risk for exposure to CMV since CMV may be contained in saliva. However, the concentration of CMV carried in the saliva of a person with an active CMV infection is believed to be generally lower than in the sperm or urine. In addition to CMV, saliva may contain other herpesviruses (such as Epstein-Barr virus which causes mononucleosis).

Kissing friends and lovers is a natural and wonderful expression of affection. Many gay men who are worried about disease are finding kissing the hardest thing to change.

Kissing with your lips closed or kissing parts of the body which do not expose you to your partner's body fluids probably poses no risk at all for CMV.

Rimming

Rimming is a high risk for CMV as well as for many other infections. Although the risk would be reduced if the partners are mutually monogamous and are certain of their good health, there is no way to make rimming risk-free. If you love to rim, consider entering a mutually monogamous relationship with a lover who has been tested.

Water Sports

Water sports can pose a grave risk to your health because urine can carry very high levels of CMV. For this reason, swallowing piss is extremely dangerous. If you must play, play it safe: aim below the neck.

Never let your partner piss into your ass. The inoculation of CMV which could result would be massive.

Dildoes

Medically safe assplay can include fingers (not fists), fucking with rubbers and dildoes. Since our primary concern here is to avoid taking in sperm and infectious agents, dildoes actually offer a relatively safe alternative to fucking if you follow certain guidelines.

Most physicians willing to discuss it recommend that the length of the dildo not exceed (approximately) 8 inches.

The dildo should be made of very soft, flexible rubber or plastic. The surface should be smooth—not defined.

Be sure that the dildo is wide enough at the base so that it won't get lost inside you.

Never use dildoes made of hard plastic, metal or which are metal-lined. Avoid dildoes which can be cranked or twisted inside you. Dildoes which are not flexible may puncture the lining of the lower intestine and cause serious injury. Never put any other objects up your ass.

Overuse of dildoes can cause inflammation. Monitor how your body responds.

Never share dildoes. Always make sure that a dildo has been disinfected before using it.

Sadism & Masochism (S & M)

S & M can involve a wide range of medically safe sexual play provided that you follow the previously mentioned guidelines for safe sexual contact and washing.

Leather, bondage, discipline, spanking, titplay, verbal, worship, teasing, affection, humiliation, gadgets, toys, etc., are some of the basics of S & M which you can do without posing any risk of disease transmission.

S & M usually begins with talking in order to determine compatibility, set limits and establish trust; this can also be the time for you and your partner to take health precautions into consideration when determining what you will or will not do.

Fist Fucking

Fist fucking can be extremely dangerous. However, fist fucking appears to have no established relationship to the development of AIDS.

Cytomegalovirus, as mentioned, may be found in the intestinal tract and it is conceivable that it could be transmitted from hands to mouth.

Washing Up

Always wash *before* sex. Showering with your partner can become an enjoyable part of foreplay.

Always wash well with soap and water immediately *after* sex.

The soap doctors and health care workers most often use is Betadine, which is available over the counter at most drug stores. Betadine is a "de-germing cleanser" that looks like and contains iodine.

Another choice is a bactericidal surgical scrub called Hibiclens which contains chlorhexadine gluconate, an anti-microbial skin cleanser. Like Betadine, these soaps can be used on a daily basis and are especially recommended if your sexual contact involves assplay. (Follow the instructions on the containers: avoid getting these soaps into your eyes and ears.)

In addition, you may also want to use PhisoHex (available only by prescription). It contains chlorine which is believed capable of killing some bacteria and amoebic cysts.

For complete and thorough washing, a fingernail scrub brush is also recommended.

Backrooms, Bookstores, Balconies, Meatracks & Tearooms

These settings permit diseases to spread like brush fire. If you have sex with someone who has just had sex with 3 partners, each of whom just had sex with 3 partners, diseases are spread exponentially. Dark settings where there are no facilities to thoroughly wash up are very dangerous places to have *any* sexual contact, let alone to have multiple sexual partners.

The Baths

As experience has taught many gay men, the bathhouses are full of disease. Often, going to the baths becomes a habit which many gay men are now finding difficult to break. One way some gay men are cutting down on their attendance is to make it a rule to always jerk off *before* you go. You may just find that it will sometimes change your mind about the "need" to go.

Having medically safe sex at the baths is definitely not practical, but this doesn't mean it isn't possible. The moment you step into a bathhouse, you are at risk for disease. But there is much you can do to minimize this risk by adopting what might be called a scientific approach to the bathhouse.

The four essential elements to this scientific approach to the baths are: talking, washing, light and rubbers.

"Been here long?" This famous bathhouse inquiry represents an unscientific attempt to determine how likely it is that a potential partner is sick. It reflects the fact that the longer a person has been at the baths, the more sex he is likely to have had; and the more sex he has had, the more likely it is that he has come into contact with diseases. In addition to asking someone if he's been here long, you should also tell him what it is you enjoy and how you plan to do it safely.

Safe sex does not require that you know your partner well, but it usually requires that you both agree before you have sex what you will and will not do. This makes it important to talk to your potential partner(s).

Talking is one way of instructing your partner about your sexual needs and can be quite erotic. If a potential partner becomes defensive or critical of your health concerns, it's probably because he feels you are implying that he might give you a disease. Since this is *exactly* what you are implying, be polite and move on.

Find a partner who will be reassured by your concerns—not put off by them. Having sex with a person who also wants to protect his health is the first step towards insuring that both you and your partner stay in control.

The importance of washing is obvious. Showers also provide an opportunity to observe a potential partner for rashes, drips, sores, sobriety, etc. Suggest showering together so that you can examine each other more closely. You don't have to be clinical. Make it a part of foreplay.

While you're showering, take the opportunity to talk about precautions and health concerns. Showering is a perfect opportunity to introduce the topic of rubbers. If all of these concerns turn him off, it's probably best to move on.

The scientific approach to the baths unfortunately means that the days of total abandon are over.

Limit yourself to one or two contacts.

Also, as part of talking, attempt to get phone numbers of your part-ners. If they won't give you their phone numbers, you can still give them yours and encourage them to contact you if any STDs develop.

As always, don't have sex with anybody unless you are sure they have washed thoroughly.

REMEMBER:

1. The moment you set foot in the bathhouse, you're at risk for disease.
2. Go with the idea that you will have no more than one or two contacts.
3. Make absolutely sure that you have inspected your part-ner's body *before* sex.
4. Make absolutely certain that both you and your partner shower well before (and after) sex.
5. Use rubbers. See that no exchange of body fluids takes place.
6. Talk about your general health and about specific limits and precautions. Be absolutely explicit.
7. Attempt to exchange phone numbers and always contact partners if symptoms develop.
8. The essence of having medically safe sex at the baths is staying in control of what you do while you are constantly being tempted into sexual abandon. The baths are an ex-tremely dangerous place to lose control, make compro-mises, or take risks with a man who *seems* healthy.

Closed Circles of Fuck Buddies

The concept of a "closed circle" of fuck buddies is merely an expanded version of monogamy. Instead of two partners, a group of partners agrees to limit all sexual contact to members of the closed group.

Clearly the safety of the entire group depends on the trustworthi-ness of each individual. The larger the group, the greater the risk that this trust will be broken.

A major advantage of a closed group of fuck buddies is that once each member has been tested beforehand for CMV and other infections, each member of the group can safely engage in any sexual act which a mutually monogamous couple might do.

Any logistical difficulties in forming and maintaining such a group might be outweighed by the variety of couplings which such a closed group would permit. This arrangement offers the variety of "promiscuity" with the safety of mutual monogamy.

The concept of a closed circle of fuck buddies is not to be confused with a sex club. Recently, a number of clubs have been formed which use various methods (such as membership buttons) to indicate an individual member's perception of the status of his health. While these clubs also rely on the trustworthiness of the members to accurately represent the healthiness of its individual members, it would probably be foolish to trust this system to protect you from disease.

Jerk-Off Clubs
Another interesting effect of the AIDS crisis has been the recent proliferation of jerk-off clubs.

J/O clubs are usually private membership clubs which require that each member agree to restrict all sexual contact to masturbation—group, mutual or self. Sucking and fucking are often prohibited and the "rules" are generally clearly posted.

Many J/O clubs provide a unique atmosphere which is friendly, communal, well-lit and intensely erotic.

The best way to find these groups is to ask around. Also, check the listings of your local bar guide or try to form your own group by placing an ad in the personal section of your local gay newspaper.

Poppers
Early in the AIDS debate, poppers—amyl and butyl nitrite—were regarded as a possible cause. As more has become known about AIDS, poppers have been pretty conclusively ruled out as the cause of AIDS.

Poppers can however cause headaches and dizziness. Poppers are poison if swallowed and can cause burns and inflammation if spilled on the skin. Never get poppers in your eyes, your mouth or your asshole.

Also, because poppers cause the blood vessels to dilate (this is the rushing sensation), they may actually facilitate the entry of microorganisms into the blood stream primarily through the lining of the ass.

The medical jury is still out on poppers. In the meantime, be aware of how your body responds if you use them and if you have any questions, talk to your doctor.

Buying Sex

Since most hustling is done in urban centers where the levels of sexually transmitted diseases are the highest, you should insist that your partner respect your health concerns. Since you are the one who is paying, it will be up to you to make sure your contact is risk free. Always talk *before* getting together about whatever precautions you plan to take. If he doesn't see that your concerns are meant to protect both of you, find someone who will.

Hustlers in any part of the country are a risk since they have sex with men from literally everywhere. Escort services—like used car salesmen—will always promise that their "models" are healthy. Because CMV and other STDs don't always produce obvious symptoms, you should apply whatever precautions are required to prevent yourself from being exposed to CMV.

Selling Sex (Hustling)

If you hustle for a living, you know that your livelihood depends on protecting your health. If you solicit through ads, you have the opportunity of stating clearly what you will and will not do, emphasizing your concern about protecting your and your partners' health.

Since hustlers are in the business of satisfying someone else's needs, you must protect yourself by setting your limits *before* you get together to have sex. This may attract the more responsible men and weed out those who may tempt you into compromising or taking health risks.

Encourage your partners to let you know if a health problem arises and you will increase the likelihood that they will.

Personals

Placing a personal ad in a gay publication is becoming a popular form of cruising in the '80s. Ads are not just for shy people. Ads allow you, quite privately, to spell out clearly any health concerns you want your potential partners to respect.

If you find that you are uncomfortable talking about health concerns face to face in a bar or bathhouse situation, ads offer an alternative method of screening out those men who do not share your health concerns.

Attracting responsible partners through an ad will make it easier for you to avoid taking risks.

Since people are not always honest, plan to meet potential partners for the first time in public places such as a bar or restaurant. Then after you meet, you have the option of going home alone or together.

Should AIDS Patients Have Sex?

This is quite a controversial issue, but regardless of what one feels, the fact is that some men who have been diagnosed with AIDS are continuing to have sex. Of course, for some AIDS patients, sex is the furthest thing from their minds. But for other AIDS patients, sexual desire remains. Some are limiting the sexual contacts they have to other AIDS patients. Others are having sex only with their lovers. And some AIDS patients are continuing to have multiple sexual contacts.

AIDS patients are human beings and need affection and human contact. AIDS patients object to being treated like lepers and some end up taking this anger and frustration out to the baths and backrooms.

The issue of AIDS patients having sex must be viewed from two perspectives: the risk to the patient and the potential risk to his partner.

The one thing AIDS patients know for sure is that they are immune suppressed. This means they are more vulnerable to infections. In addition, if they *do* develop an infection, they know that they will have a more difficult time recovering. It is possible that sex is more of a danger to the AIDS patient than to his partner. Considering the risks to the patients themselves, multiple sexual contacts, particularly in settings such as the baths and backrooms where disease is rampant, is extremely unwise.

In terms of the risk to the partners of AIDS patients, we believe that the primary danger is the transmission of CMV. Of course, if you believe that there is a new virus which is the cause of AIDS, having sex with an AIDS patient might transmit such a new virus.

The decision of whether and how AIDS patients should have sex and the decisions of whether and how partners should have sex with AIDS patients are difficult ones to make. Each person must weigh the evidence, determine his own risk, and act accordingly. However, WE BELIEVE THAT AIDS PATIENTS HAVE AN ETHICAL OBLIGATION TO AD-VISE POTENTIAL PARTNERS OF THEIR HEALTH STATUS.

We believe that AIDS patients must allow their potential partners to make their own choice. There *are* gay men who are willing to have sex with AIDS patients and who are willing to take the necessary precautions designed to protect both partners' health. Obviously, we believe that lovers of AIDS patients may continue having sex with AIDS patients if they exercise the precautions outlined in this paper. There are AIDS patients who are continuing to have "safe sex" and who are recovering from their immune suppression. And there are lovers who have continued to have sex safely with AIDS patients who are not showing signs of immune deficiency and who are not contracting CMV.

But apart from the issue of sex, in the absence of firm evidence that AIDS can be transmitted by casual, non-sexual intimacy, we see no reason why hugging and affection should be discouraged or withheld.

Guilt, Morality and Sex Negativity

The AIDS crisis has forced many gay men to examine their lifestyles. It has also produced a lot of recommendations which are really misplaced morality masquerading as medical advice.

Gay men have always been criticized for having "too much sex" with "too many" different partners. Because the development of AIDS in gay men is obviously somehow connected with the amount and kind of sex we have, a lot of advice has focused on "reducing" the "number of different partners". Wherever we turn we are reminded of the joys of romance and dating by those who claim they are only concerned with our health.

In this age of AIDS, the advice most often given is that we should try to "cut down" on the number of different partners we have sex with, and try to limit those partners we do have sex with to "healthy" men. This advice confuses many gay men. What is meant by "cut down"? Is it going to the baths once a month instead of once a week? Is it having two partners a night instead of four? And how can we determine whether or not a potential partner is "healthy" when there are many infections which don't have obvious symptoms? While having less sex will definitely reduce our chances for all STDs, it will certainly not eliminate them.

Advice which focuses only on *numbers* and which ignores ways to interrupt disease transmission is incomplete. For example, a gay man who is concerned with protecting his health may decide to "cut down" on the amount of sex he has by limiting himself to one different partner a month. At the end of the year, he will have had sex with 12 different partners. Few gay men would consider having 12 sex partners a year being "promiscuous," but this example illustrates the point that the issue isn't sex, it's disease. Since one out of every four of his 12 sexual partners was probably contagious for CMV (despite his best efforts to guess who was "healthy"), he will have been exposed to CMV 3 times that year—unless he limited which sexual acts he performed to ones which interrupt disease transmission.

If a concerned gay man makes the tremendous effort to change his sexual behavior by reducing the number of different partners, yet fails to modify what he does, chances are high that he will still often get sick. This has to be demoralizing. He may even feel that all his efforts have been useless and go back to his old patterns. Or he may respond by giving up sex completely.

But deciding to stop having sex because sex may lead to AIDS is not the same as deciding to stop smoking because smoking can cause cancer. Smoking is a habit, a luxury, a "vice." Sex is a natural and important human need. Although every individual will ultimately have to balance need and risk himself, to do so will require that he have the information necessary to make informed changes.

And while we're on the subject, what's all this talk about "anonymous" sex being dangerous? Anonymity in itself has nothing to do with disease transmission.

If your partner introduces himself, he is no longer an anonymous partner. But if he's contagious for syphilis, you'll get syphilis. It's as simple as that.

A lot of this talk about "anonymous" sex being "bad" smacks of misplaced morality. The issue is disease—not sex.

One reason why anonymity can be dangerous is that when you don't know your partners, you may not be as cautious in protecting him from disease. We need a more precise vocabulary to talk about the various lifestyles we lead.

When you are receiving advice about sex, it's very important to make sure that the advice is based on sound, scientific understanding of how diseases are transmitted. Don't be fooled just because the source of advice seems authoritative. Verify what you are told by talking to physicians and consulting other sources of information.

If we are to celebrate our gayness and get on with gay liberation, we must stay healthy. To stay healthy, we must realize that the issue isn't gayness or sex; the issue is simply disease.

Love

It came as quite a shock to us to find that we had written almost 40 pages on sex without mentioning the word "love" once. Truly, we have been revealed as products of the '70s.

It has become unfashionable to refer to sex as "love-making." Why might this be so?

If the sexual revolution that began in the '60s confirmed one thing it was that sex and affection—sex and love—are not necessarily the same thing. The concept of "recreational sex" has gained widespread acceptance.

At the same time, as the rising epidemics of STDs have demonstrated, there are certain unfortunate (and unforeseen?) side effects when love and affection become so separated from sex.

Without affection, it is less likely that you will care as much if you give your partners disease. During the '70s fantasy was encouraged. Sex with partners you did not know—and did not want to know—was justified as being personally meaningful even if it wasn't interpersonally so. Put another way, did gay male culture of the '70s encourage us to substitute the *fantasy* of the man we were holding for his reality?

Gay men are socialized as men first; our gay socialization comes later. From the day we are born we are trained as men to compete with other men. The challenge facing gay men in America is to figure out how to love someone you've been trained to "destroy."

The goal of gay male liberation must be to find ways in which love becomes possible despite continuing and often overwhelming pressure to compete and adopt adversary relationships with other men.

Gay male politics have historically suffered from fractionalism. Might this be a symptom of the competitiveness between males? And why has it been so difficult to involve gay men politically? Is it possible that all this great sex we've been having for the last decade has siphoned off our collective anger which might otherwise have been translated into social and political action?

The commercialization of urban gay male culture today offers us places to go and get sick and places to go and get treated. Too many gay man get together for only two reasons: to exploit each other and to be exploited.

Sex and "promiscuity" have become the dogma of gay male liberation. Have we modified the belief that we could dance our way to liberation into the belief that we could somehow fuck our way there? If sex is liberating, is more sex necessarily more liberating?

It has certainly become easier to fuck each other. But has it become any easier to love each other? Men *loving* men was the basis of gay male liberation, but we have now created "cultural institutions" in which love or even affection can be totally avoided.

If you love the person you are fucking with—*even for one night*—you will not want to make them sick.

Maybe affection is our best protection.

Hard questions for hard times. But whatever happened to our great gay imaginations?

Some Closing Thoughts

The party that was the '70s is over. Taking ignorance to the baths and backrooms is not sexual freedom—it's oppression.

Not all gay men are well-educated and well-off; not all gay men can afford the benefits of proper health care. What we as a community must do is to make available vital information about how diseases are transmitted so that each of us can make *informed* decisions about our lives. If AIDS proves to be the result of the epidemic rise of CMV and other common infections, the AIDS crisis may prove to have been a crystal clear reflection of just how little we knew about protecting our health.

What's over isn't sex—just sex without responsibility.

HOW TO HAVE SEX IN AN EPIDEMIC:
One Approach
by: Richard Berkowitz & Michael Callen
With Editorial Assistance by:
Richard Dworkin

Praise for
How to Have Safe Sex in an Epidemic

"This is the sanest, most sensible advice I've read yet about AIDS."

—EDMUND WHITE, Author,
The Joy of Gay Sex, States of Desire.

"At last: a response to the effect of AIDS on our lives that goes beyond fears and myths to suggest positive actions."

—DENNIS ALTMAN, Author,
The Homosexualization of America, Coming Out in the 70s.

"Particularly well-done. . . "

—THE VILLAGE VOICE

"It urges a sensible restriction of sex among currently promiscuous homosexual males. . . "

—THE NEW YORK REVIEW OF BOOKS

"Every homosexual in America should immediately order this booklet. It'll be the best $3.75 you ever spent."

—STALLION

"An extraordinarily intelligent and provocative booklet."

—DRUMMER

"The only literature yet produced by this particular crisis in human affairs, is this touchingly funny, very instructive 40-page pamphlet. . . "

—PETER FISHER, Author,
AIDS: Your Questions Answered

219

"The useful thing about it is that it is precisely about how to have sex, not a warning not to. . . "

—THE BODY POLITIC

"Presents a sensible way of dealing with anxiety by trying to understand the situation and by living with it as sensibly as possible. . . "

—DUNGEONMASTER

"Sympathetic. . . their recommendations are appropriate for all sexually active gay men. . . "

—GARY STEELE, Editor, FRONTIERS

1984—GAY PRESS ASSOCIATION AWARD for "Outstanding Community Project"

CMV Update
In a recently published study entitled "Cytomegalovirus Infections in Homosexual Men," researcher W. Lawrence Drew and colleagues conclude that "Primary infection with CMV can suppress cell-mediated immunity, and repeated exposure to this virus could result in a protracted state of immunosuppression. In such a case, CMV infection could play a central role in initiating the acquired immunodeficiency syndrome afflicting homosexual men."

Drew's study of 237 gay men discovered that a staggering 35% (one out of *three*) of those tested were actively excreting CMV in their sperm. To find out why some of the men developed CMV while others did not, Drew studied seven different sexual practices: sucking, getting sucked, fucking, getting fucked, rimming, getting rimmed and kissing. Drew found that "Of seven sexual practices investigated, only passive anal/genital intercourse (getting fucked) correlated with the acquisition of CMV infection." We believe that Drew's findings make one thing absolutely clear: GAY MEN IN SETTINGS WHERE CMV IS PREVALENT WHO ARE CONTINUING TO GET FUCKED WITHOUT TAKING PRECAUTIONS ARE PLACING THEIR HEALTH IN GRAVE DANGER.

Those interested in reading the full report of Dr. Drew and his colleagues should consult the September *Annals of Internal Medicine* (1983; 99:326–329).

How to Use This Booklet

In the foreword to the first edition of this booklet, Dr. Sonnabend correctly pointed out that our guidelines were not intended to be "an encouragement of promiscuity." Based on feedback which we have received from those who have attempted to follow our guidelines, we have decided that it is necessary to amplify and modify a few points:

1. "THE MOMENT YOU STEP INTO A BATHHOUSE YOU ARE AT RISK FOR DISEASE." We want to make one thing absolutely clear: WE DO NOT RECOMMEND THAT ANY-ONE HAVE SEX IN A BATHHOUSE, particularly in those cities where staggering rates of CMV infection are being documented. Although we believe that those who are continuing to have sex in bathhouses can *reduce* their risk, our guidelines are *not* intended in any sense to be an encouragement of bathhouse sexual activity.

2. REDUCE YOUR NUMBER OF DIFFERENT PARTNERS. We have come to recognize that our advice didn't sufficiently emphasize the human error factor. Of course, if everyone successfully interrupted disease transmission by following our guidelines, it wouldn't matter how many different partners they had. But of course, people make mistakes: condoms break, coitus interruptus isn't always interrupted, etc. That is why we recommended on page xx that those who are continuing to have sex in bathhouses should "Limit yourself to one or two contacts." Even though we do NOT believe that AIDS can result from a *single,* unlucky contact, each mistake—each reinfection with CMV—can have serious and cumulative consequences. Reducing your number of partners is particularly important in settings like bathhouses where the levels of CMV and other diseases are so high. REMEMBER: The

fewer different partners you have, the less chance you will have of making a mistake.

3. "IF YOU LOVE THE PERSON YOU'RE FUCKING WITH—EVEN FOR ONE NIGHT—YOU WILL NOT WANT TO MAKE THEM SICK. AFFECTION IS OUR BEST PROTECTION." Because we were overly sensitive to charges of being "judgmental," we avoided stressing the best and most obvious solution to the issue of sex in the age of AIDS: mutual monogamy. Those who have found lovers deserve all the encouragement and support we can offer. Aside from the issue of disease, there are many advantages to love and intimacy which we should not be embarrassed to acknowledge. Put another way:

SEX IS WONDERFUL!
RESERVE IT FOR THOSE YOU LOVE AND TRUST!

M. Callen, R. Berkowitz
December 1983

Condom Update

The recent controversy in the gay community concerning the effectiveness of condoms as a barrier to the transmission of viruses must be addressed. There is no good evidence that viruses are capable of passing through latex (rubbers). This is best explained this way: If you fill a condom with water it will hold the water inside. Since virus particles such as herpes simplex or cytomegalovirus are thousands of times larger than water molecules, there is no basis for suggesting that viruses can pass through latex.

HOWEVER, RUBBERS CAN ONLY PROTECT YOU IF YOU USE THEM PROPERLY. The reason why manufacturers of condoms and the physicists who design them cannot guarantee 100% protection is because rubbers are open-ended and may slip off or rip *if improperly used.*

NEVER USE PETROLEUM-BASED LUBRICANTS WHEN USING CONDOMS MADE OF LATEX. Petroleum-based lubricants can dissolve latex and might allow infectious agents to pass through the dissolving latex.

Some men have learned the hard way that it is possible for condoms to rip in the heat of passion—or worse—at the moment of climax. For gay men who live in high-risk urban areas, the best way to insure protection is *not* to let your partner come inside you even if he *is* wearing a rubber.

THERE CAN BE NO EQUIVOCATION: SHORT OF SEXUAL AB-STINENCE, RUBBERS PROVIDE SEXUALLY ACTIVE GAY MEN WITH THE BEST PROTECTION CURRENTLY AVAILABLE. To discourage their use by those who have decided to continue sexual activity during this health crisis verges on the irresponsible.

Notes

Chapter 1

1. (New York: David McKay, 1969), pp. 162, 176–177.

Chapter 2

1. Toby Marotta, *The Politics of Homosexuality* (Boston: Houghton Mifflin, 1981), p. ix.

2. Barbara Ehrenreich, E. Hess, G. Jacobs, et al., *Re-Making Love: The Feminization of Sex* (New York: Anchor Books, 1986), pp. 71–77.

3. Gore Vidal, *United States* (New York: Random House, 1993), p. 368.

4. Carole S. Vance, ed. (New York: Routledge, 1984).

5. James Tyson, "Toward a New Gay Morality," *Blueboy*, vol. 25, October 1978, pp. 3, 17, 19.

Chapter 4

1. "AIDS and the Question of an Infectious Agent," *New York Native*, pp. 21, 49, September 13–26, 1982.

2. Gay Men's Health Crisis newsletter, no. 1, July 1982, pp. 30–33.

3. "T-Cell Ratios in Homosexual Men," *The Lancet*, April 17, 1982, 1:908.

4. This was the beginning of the American Foundation for AIDS research, known today as AmFar.

5. "From Gay Ghetto to Gay Community," a New School course taught by writer Edmund White in 1982.

6. Issue 63, vol. 6, no. 3.

Epilogue

1. (London: Cassell, 1993; New York: Routledge, 1994).

Bibliography

Several books were influential in either shaping or clarifying my understanding and the ideas that are expressed in this book. By acknowledging them I do not wish to imply that any of the authors cited endorse what I've written; some may very well be at odds with it. Many books and essays by Gore Vidal and Barbara Ehrenreich have been invaluable to me in making sense of life in America, but I include only two books by Ehrenreich in this short bibliography.

Brody, Stuart. *Sex at Risk: Lifetime Number of Partners, Frequency of Intercourse, and the Low AIDS Risk of Vaginal Intercourse.* New Brunswick, NJ: Transaction Publishers, 1997.

Ehrenreich, Barbara, and D. English. *For Her Own Good: 150 Years of the Experts Advice to Women.* New York: Anchor Books, 1979.

Ehrenreich, Barbara, E. Hess, and G. Jacobs. *Re-Making Love: The Feminization of Sex.* New York: Anchor Books, 1986.

Illich, Ivan. *Medical Nemesis: The Expropriation of Health.* New York: Random House, 1976.

King, Edward. *Safety in Numbers: Safer Sex and Gay Men.* London: Cassell, 1993; New York: Routledge 1994.

Marotta, Toby. *The Politics of Homosexuality: How Lesbians and Gay Men Have Made Themselves a Political and Social Force in Modern America.* Boston: Houghton Mifflin, 1981.

Patterson, James, and P. Kim. *The Day America Told the Truth.* New York: Plume, 1992.

Reuben, David, M.D. *Everything You Always Wanted to Know about Sex but Were Afraid to Ask.* New York: Bantam Books / David McKay, 1970.

Rushing, William A. *The AIDS Epidemic: Social Dimensions of an Infectious Disease.* Boulder, CO: Westview Press, 1995.

Vance, Carole S., ed. *Pleasure and Danger: Exploring Female Sexuality.* London: Pandora Press, 1989.

Wagner, Jane. *The Search for Signs of Intelligent Life in the Universe.* New York: HarperPerennial, 1986.

White, Edmund. *States of Desire, Travels in Gay America.* New York: Penguin Books, 1991.

Index